COACHING YOUTH BASKETBALL

A GUIDE FOR FIRST-TIMERS

SECOND EDITION

BY
STUART WADE

Coaching Youth Basketball: A Guide for First-Timers

Copyright © 2022 by Stuart Wade

Published by North Fir Communications. All rights reserved. No part of this book may be reproduced or transmitted in any form or by any means without written permission from the author.

For Christi, Ben, John & Rob — I love you guys!

INTRODUCTION
YOU GOT THE JOB. NOW WHAT?

It's a common tale. After a YMCA soccer season during which my second grader participated, he and his teammates approached their soccer coach. "We want to play Y basketball," they said, asking if he would oversee them.

Possessing plenty of soccer — but not basketball — knowledge, our coach deferred to team parents. "The boys want to play basketball together," he told us. "If anyone wants to coach them this winter, let me know."

Having grown up with 'Midwestern basketball DNA,' I approached him. "I can assist whoever decides to do it," I suggested to him. "No one came forward," he told me. "Congratulations — Coach!"

What had I gotten myself into? Sure, I understood the rules and had been a longtime spectator. That did not, however, qualify me to teach, manage a gaggle of kids, or understand strategic points of the game well enough to translate, motivate and inspire others.

Who was I kidding?

That was 15 basketball seasons ago. Since that time, I have coached or otherwise overseen hundreds of basketball players between the ages of 6 and 18. I've worked with a half-dozen organizations and approximately 30 different basketball groups over that span (occasionally coaching multiple teams in a season). Leagues ranged from purely recreation, to a dedicated, 800-player youth basketball league that I helped administrate, and on to private AAU basketball traveling teams competing at some of the highest levels of youth hoops.

Apart from my being a husband and father (and enjoying career successes), coaching youth basketball has turned out to be one of the more rewarding (and unexpected) highlights of my adult life. And it's all because I took that first, terrifying step and agreed to coach when I knew next to nothing about it.

The purpose of this book is to let you know that you can take that step.

FOREWORD

<u>by Steven Dietz</u>

Though I am long removed from my days as an athlete, I can still spot a person who played competitive sports in their youth. I saw it in my students at the University of Texas at Austin, those who had an uncanny ability to rebound from adversity with grit and resilience. I'm convinced all our Saturday mornings on the basketball court (or the baseball/soccer field) start us on the road toward life's most necessary lessons: preparation, commitment, discipline, positive attitude, mental toughness, responsibility, generosity. And if, in those formative years, we are lucky enough to have a coach like Stuart Wade, all the better. My son Abraham was one of those lucky kids. He learned invaluable lessons from "Coach Wade": lessons about basketball, teamwork, accountability, and sportsmanship. Any reader of <u>Coaching Youth Basketball</u> is destined to learn the same – all of it delivered with Stuart's trademark cordiality, candor and Hoosier Pride.

Coaches have an enormous impact on young people, and on the adults those young people become. Stuart Wade knows this well. His keen and clear understanding of the "hardware" of coaching (practices, plays, strategies), as well as the "software" of coaching (dealing with parents, disappointments, expectations), is on full display in these pages. I believe this welcome, timely, and necessary book is destined to become a go-to resource for both the first-time youth basketball coach, and the more experienced coach looking to refresh or refine their approach.

Organized as a road map from First Meeting to Final Game, this book gives clear, practical and game-ready advice on offensive sets, defensive schemes, clock management, and substitution patterns, among other tangible tools. Aware that every coach will find the approach that suits them and their team, Stuart wisely offers multiple templates (for both practices and games) that can be employed and adapted, as needed. Perhaps the most challenging part of being a youth coach is meeting each player at their individual skill level. Stuart advises his coaching brethren to embrace this challenge, while offering time-tested strategies on how to coach *in* a system while coaching *to* your player.

Younger kids typically begin playing basketball in that sweet spot between having fun, learning a sport, getting some exercise, and enjoying a snack. This is where Stuart's coaching began (as his own sons were that age), and that is where this book begins. The lessons to be learned at this age are huge and invaluable – and Stuart handles them as an author in the same way he did as a coach: with grace, clarity, and forward-leaning optimism. I can still hear him calling out to a dejected player after a missed shot or turnover: "Next play! Defend the lane! Keep moving!"

As players' ages and abilities grow, this book provides a comprehensive coaching tool-kit (strategies, games plans, terminology) that will grow right along with them. What's more: Stuart is bracingly candid about managing both player and parental expectations at the middle-school level, where the gulf begins to widen between those who are "competitively-directed" and those onboard for the social benefits of being on a team. Youth sports can and must accommodate both these outlooks, however the "Coach" is often the person charged with striking that complicated balance between making champions and making memories. Stuart has filled this book with personal anecdotes about being a coach in that challenging position. His insights and tangible suggestions are hopeful, revealing and deeply instructive.

Finally, Stuart infuses this book with unexpected gems: how to deal with bad calls by referees, parents who want to coach from the stands, overly-aggressive players on the other team. A particular favorite of mine is a transcript of what to say to a team after a season which produced only *one victory*. As one of Stuart's assistant coaches, I was there when he made this speech. My son was on that team. Though Abraham was also on Stuart's teams that went on to win tournaments and championships, I remember that year – and that speech – above all. Kneeling in front of a throng of sweaty, exhausted, dispirited 7th graders, Stuart managed to give them not something to regret, but something to *build upon*.

*With **Coaching Youth Basketball**, Stuart Wade is doing the same for you. He is making you ready to be a coach on your own. Humble to a fault, Stuart doesn't want the bucket – he wants the assist. He wants you to take the shot. I can hear him on the sidelines, calling out: "Go for it! And then get back on Defense!"*

Steven Dietz
Steven Dietz is a playwright, theatre director, and former *professor at UT/Austin.*

CONTENTS

INTRODUCTION | YOU GOT THE "JOB." NOW WHAT? i

FOREWORD iii

1 | OFF THE COURT 1

2 | GET ORGANIZED 9

3 | PREPARING 19

4 | GAME TIME 53

5 | MIDDLE SCHOOL 105

6 | PLAYS 127

OVERTIME 139

ABOUT THE AUTHOR 153

ACKNOWLEDGMENTS 155

1
OFF THE COURT

"First, master the fundamentals."

-LARRY BIRD

AGES: DEVELOPMENT and FORMATS

Note: The path we followed, 2006-2021, is an approximation to national standards. Your league rules may vary.

The NBA and USA Basketball have issued age-range guidelines that break down the age ranges by: 7-8, 9-11 and 12-14 here:

• https://youthguidelines.nba.com

Handy ball and goal specifications here:

• https://www.nba.com/news/nba-usa-basketball-youth-basketball-rules

NOVICE - Under 6

Emphasis is on learning fundamentals, movements and motor skills

- Games played on shorter 8-foot goals, using Size 3 (22-inch circumference) ball
- Introduction to team principles/concepts
- Group skills clinics are recommended

Ages 7-8

We played YMCA. Games for this age range are played across a standard-size court, with lowered goals.

- Junior size Size 5 ball (27.5-inch); 8-foot goals

- All-equal playing rotations

- Typically, man-to-man only (no zone) where you matchup via same-color wristband

- Often no score is kept. (Trust me, the kids will know the score)

INTERMEDIATE - Ages 9-10

- Play cross court (2 baskets across width of a standard full court)

- Junior size 6 ball (28.5-inch); 9-foot goals

- No score is kept; no free throws and no fouls kept (The players will know the score!)

- 8-minute quarters, clock runs continuously, 2 timeouts per half. No OT

- Play man-to-man only (no zone), defender must stay 3 feet away

Ages 11-12

- 10-foot goals and play FULL court... lots more running

- Junior size 6 ball (28.5)

- Scoring is kept; fouls and foul shots, too

- Man-to-man only, steal off the pass only

- 8-minute quarters, clock runs continuously (has an overtime)

- May press conditionally, e.g., late in game and/or picking up at 3/4 court (opposition foul line)

ADVANCED - Ages 12-14

At this age we moved to NWAYBA, a PCA sanctioned open K-12 league

- Full court, official-size basketball (29.5 inches), 10-foot goals

- Tryout and team selection

- All defenses; exception if a 12-point lead, No Pressing

- 15-minute halves with Stop clock; 4 TOs per game

WHY BE A COACH?

Basketball is a grand game; what you're willing to put in will come back to you a thousand times over.

There are many great reasons to say "Yes," when you've been asked to coach.

- You get to pass along knowledge, teach basic skills to some great kids, and meet terrific parents, all centered around a game that's fun to play
- It's a golden opportunity to put young people into position to develop lifelong values, such as teamwork and perseverance
- Youth hoops gives youngsters a lot more than how to shoot a basketball; playing the sport together helps kids develop in maturity and gives them confidence

Your decisions and outlook influence the players' attitudes, their approach to group dynamics and individual effort, and how they feel about basketball later. Sure, there are life lessons: leadership, the importance of hard work, and sacrifice for a common goal.

There is competition, too, no question about it. However, for the majority of your young charges, playing the game of basketball will only be a brief part of growing up. Your job is to help those players have so much fun playing basketball this season, that they will return enthusiastically for the next one.

The Changing the Game Project says coaches are accountable in the following ways:

- Treat them with respect and encourage them as they learn
- Be a positive role model
- Be a clear, consistent communicator and listener
- Make it normal to fail and learn
- Remember, it's all for the kids

Ultimately, coaching is about building relationships and being a positive force in the well-being of young people. Coaching is a responsibility and a privilege. Enjoy every minute…

Say, "YES!"

2
GET ORGANIZED

"Plans are nothing; planning is everything."

-DWIGHT EISENHOWER

FIRST THINGS FIRST

A few weeks before the actual coaching can begin, you will perform a few administrative tasks:

- Secure your group or team's participation in the league
- Establish good communication with [and a primary contact person from] the league
- Contact all families in your group, trying to get a feel for the commitment level of each individual family

Typically, in youth basketball, you play one game per week and practice once weekly. As age ranges advance, expect two to three weekly "meetings" (longer practices and more games).

Some parents will jump in right away and offer their time and energy to help in any way they can. For various reasons, others you may rarely see, even at games. Mention often how your families may help you, with working the scoreboard, scorebook, driving/sharing rides, providing snacks, helping with the uniforms, etc. Get an early idea regarding who's in which category.

Assessing the ability of each child to attend your team's games and practices is crucial, too. If a particular child/family can't make it, try to find out why and offer to arrange rides, etc. While winning isn't "priority one" when you're coaching a team of 7-year-olds, at the same time, it's not fair to those who come to every practice to reward those who don't show up that often (or at all).

OVER-COMMUNICATE

You must communicate well and often with your group of parents. Get help if you aren't good at this by identifying and assigning a "Team Parent."

The first note you will send to the overall group is to introduce yourself, share contacts for your players' parents, and practice information. In addition, this communication will help you identify your team parent (see next section) and find potential candidates for assistant coaching.

You should also consider who from the new "family" might be your primary parents who will look after the clock and scorebook duties during games if the league doesn't already provide them.

NAME A TEAM PARENT

Your first action is to identify this individual! The team parent serves as the central point of contact for the Coach to coordinate off-the-court team matters with the overall group of parents. Typically, the team parent will help you spread the administrative workload, freeing the coaching role so you can focus more on basketball.

Team Parents' primary responsibilities include assisting in communication (calls/emails/texts/group texts) with parents and taking the lead in confirming player availability for practices and games. Some team parents also help coordinate uniforms and team photos.

It's not a bad idea to have a parent volunteer tracking simple hustle stats — rebounds, forced jump balls and turnovers —

even if the league provides fully-paid scoring table personnel; or if it keeps no scores at all. Here's a link, active as of September 2022, to a downloadable hustle-stats sheet: https://bit.ly/3RcPQtH .

Bonus half-time thought: Often if we were losing or just needed a spark, I'd call over the hustle-stats parent and have him or her read who has the most rebounds, steals, deflections, etc. Motivation is where you find it!

Perhaps most importantly for younger players, the Team Parent should coordinate the post-game snack schedule and ensure that at every game (and practice, if desired) a parent/family contributes a post-game refreshment or snack.

ESSENTIALS: CHECKLISTS FOR A FIRST-TIME COACH

PRACTICE CHECKLIST

Agenda/script for that practice A whistle

Practice mesh jerseys (aka "Pinnies")

Training items — Cones, agility ladder, small hurdles for drills (enough for minimum of 8-10 participants)

Basketballs and basketball goals that meet your league standards (Typically, a "junior" sized basketball for ages under 10; 10-foot goals are standard, and some leagues lower the goals to 9- or even 8-feet)

Practice snack rotation

GAME CHECKLIST

Player rotation specific for that game

Balls

Uniforms/league jerseys

Bench assistant coach - HUGE!

Dry-erase basketball clipboard and marker (You'll know you're "locked in" as a youth coach when the glovebox of your vehicle starts filling with dry-erase markers)

Game snack rotation

Score/clock parent volunteers (if not already provided by your league)

LEAGUE CHECKLIST

League schedule & rules, player roster and fees, practice schedule, uniform & fee

Regular practice day(s) and time(s)

Practice venue directions; game venue directions

Parent contact info including mobile numbers and email addresses for -all- parents of a given player

Rules and officiating contact/liaison – contact information

EMAIL EXAMPLE: PRESEASON "INTRO" TO YOUR TEAM

Hello, my name is [NAME] and I am looking forward to serving as your coach for YMCA Winter Hoops! We're still awaiting information -- game and practice schedules, official rosters and team name -- from the league. Here's the current link on the YMCA site [LINK]

If you would like to serve as an assistant coach, please let me know! Likewise, we need a team parent to help the coaches set up refreshment schedules, help with uniforms, communications, and much more.

KEY UPCOMING DATES

Saturday, January 3 (11 a.m.) - **Pre-season pizza/shootaround at COACH'S**

My address: 1234 Main, (xxx)yyy-yyyy

- Informal get-together for those who can make it; ending around 1pm

- We will pass out team jersey/shirts (if ready). If you cannot attend, I will bring shirts to our first week practices and game

- Come one, come all!

TBD weeknight, most likely Saturday, Jan 8 but not yet confirmed - First **YMCA indoor practice at [LOCATION]**

- Update coming to all as soon as we hear

- For practice, please have your child bring a ball

Saturday, January 10 (time TBD) - **First game of the season [LOCATION]**

-Please arrive 10-15 minutes early for warm up/shooting on the shorter goals

-Please familiarize yourselves and the guys with location of the first-floor YMCA bathroom/drinking fountain & please encourage a pregame bathroom break

POSTGAME SNACK SCHEDULE

- 1/10 - Coach Wade
- 1/17 - Smith
- 1/24 - Jones
- 1/31 - Johnson
- 2/7 - open [please sign up]
- 2/14 - open
- 2/21 - open
- 2/28 - open

All are welcome to sign on for later snacks (reply to this e-mail), and I'll add your name to the memo. THANKS to all parent volunteers.

YOUR NAME

Phone/contact info

PS - For those who've asked -- some noteworthy rules information re both leagues:

- We'll play cross court (2 baskets across width of standard full court)
- Junior size ball; 8.5- or 9-foot goals; rims are larger
- No fouls will be kept (no foul shots)
- Man-to-man only, defenders must stay "3 feet" away
- 8-minute quarters, clock runs continuously. No overtime--we'll sub full squads, frequently
- Defensive matchups are assigned, using colored wristbands, by coaches/refs

Get your guys thinking about hoops this week! Thanks

SAMPLE TEAM PARENT TEXT

Hello everyone,

I will be team parent for the [NICKNAME] team. For returning parents and players, it's great to have you back — For everyone else, <u>WELCOME</u>!

- **Our first practice will be Thursday, January 8, from 10-11 a.m. at [LOCATION]**
- Looks like we will be practicing at this location and time every Thursday. We'll keep you posted if that changes
- Bring water and a ball - wear white tee shirt, Coach will have practice jerseys/"pinnies"

Note re: League jerseys: In a few days I expect to share with everyone the league's sizing chart PDF for you to look over and get us the sizing asap (and your preferred jersey NUMBER).

No league shorts are being issued — So for games, please have you child wear black (or dark) shorts.

Looking forward to an exciting season!

[Team parent NAME]

[Team parent PHONE NUMBER]

3
PREPARING

"I'm a very positive thinker, and I think that is what helps me the most in difficult moments."

-ROGER FEDERER, 8-TIME WIMBLEDON CHAMPION

LET'S MEET YOUR TEAM

Before you take the floor for the very first time, it's likely you'll already know some, a majority, or all of the players/families assigned to your team.

A few of your players will already be active in basketball. Others will have played some basketball already, and a few may have never picked up a ball.

Likewise, their parents will bring a range of expectations to their child's basketball season. Some will be wanting their kids to compete and win, rooting hard at every game, others are simply grateful for a new physical fitness and social outlet for their child.

Take stock of your group to quickly assess where they all are on the basketball "adoption curve." Your job is to make it a fun and rewarding experience for all.

PARENT MEETING: DAY ONE MATERIAL

- Advocate good sportsmanship as your Number One Rule. It comes above all else. Walk in on Day One teaching your kids, "Honor The Game." Which means, we respect one another and the officials. In games and practices, we go hard but always remember to treat our teammates and opponents the right way. We also play the right way: we never demean the opponent, complain, or run up the score. Wins and losses are secondary to teamwork, helping one another and encouraging every person. We are in this together.

- Patient coaching and acceptance of each child on his/her own skill level is an equally important Day One point to make. It's going to be okay to make mistakes...We're going to make them and learn together.

- Be honest and open with your parents from Day One and make yourself available to talk and answer questions before and after events. Team decision-making rests with you, but you're open to their comments. It doesn't mean you have to alter your game plan. Take the lead. And remember that you need them, as they need you. Make it a dialog... just not a democracy.

- Parents need to be aware not to "coach from the stands." Promote the importance of one voice their children hear when it comes to Xs and Os. Especially at the earliest ages, the parents' "job" is to cheer plays and players.

I'm tacking on this gem of a quote, paraphrased from the Harvey Dorfman book, *Coaching the Mental Game*:

"As any coach knows, there are great parents too — great for their kids, great for the coach, great for the sport. What more can coaches do than appreciate these people — and convey this appreciation? It is no coincidence that their children are also great to coach, with very few exceptions. I used great parents as conduits for not-so-great parents. It saved me, when another approach didn't bring results. When that didn't work, I handed the situation directly."

PLAYERS, ALL TYPES

Figure out your skill players. Those who are good at handling the ball or shooting will be your guards or your wings. Your post players are the rebounding specialists (often, but not always, the bigger players). At this age the traditional basketball 1-5 positions don't mean a whole lot, BUT you do come across instances when a player who is "supposed to" be playing the 4 (forward) or 5 (center) wants to be the 1 (point guard).

This will be someone who wants to bring the ball up court, but isn't quite as skillful as others in that role. Your job is to end this, but also to retain the trust of this certain someone whom you see being more successful as a "big." During games you're going to want to get 80-plus percent of your team's ballhandling done by the better dribblers. Weaker handle, but guard-sized, kids can play wing.

Do not overlook the teammates who — while they may not yet possess dribble or shooting skill — are athletic, hustling types. These are often highly coachable players whose floor-diving, assertive efforts will become contagious. You'll love these battlers and scrappers. And finally, you will have novice players who are just as much a part of the attack as your most seasoned youth-hoop "veterans." Make them all feel welcome and part of the plan.

PRACTICE - EARLY "PRE-PREP"

Keep it simple: You'll be amazed how quickly an hour passes. You only have 60 minutes, maybe up to 90 minutes if you're lucky. So, it's crucial to keep things simple, scripted and moving right along. Structure and organize those difference-making drills and scrimmages beforehand.

Get organized: Much of your overall coaching success depends on how well organized you are, how much time and energy you can devote to preparation. This includes running a crisp, productive practice.

PRE-PREP: THE DAY BEFORE

- List what you want to cover and schedule your rundown *to the minute* (at the actual practice, have your assistant or an attending parent help you with the time schedule)

- Simplicity and repetition are your allies for effective instruction. Positive language ("Try it this way") over negative language.

- <u>You must begin with the fundamentals</u>: Every season, every age group — start that first sessions together with dribbling, ball-handling, passing and simple defensive fundamentals drills, which not only will help "young motors" warm to basketball motor skills they'll need over the next hour, but also will give you a glimpse into where kids are on the "curve."

Dribbling is the basic skill in basketball. Start with this baseline to assess where your players are on adoption and mastery, and adjust your lessons accordingly. At the outset of coaching/playing the sport, you will have players who may need to spend a lot more time simply dribbling. That's perfectly normal.

A quick note on drills: Make them fun. Young players I coached loved drills and we always tried to identify which ones were popular, mixing in the more challenging ones.

Passing drills - sharp/crisp chest, bounce and overhead passes; Ball fake, then pass ball. (The bounce pass is a high-value asset – find your bounce-passers)

- Limit any single drill to a maximum of 3-4 minutes. Young players have short attention spans

- Drilling *shooting* at a practice is less important than you'd think. Shooting is the one thing the kids ARE doing away from you; better to devote precious practice time to learning other basic hoops/coordination skills

- Pro tip: Allow only one basketball on the court during spoken instruction; no dribbling until told "OK"

- When installing an offensive concept, often you may wish to have five defenders out there, too, even if they aren't active in the instruction. (You want to involve as many players at a time as you can, and you can then "flip it" to put defenders on offense and show them the given set or play)

• Do your best to work through your agenda quickly. Gauge player comprehension, body language: If the majority "Get It," move to the next item. Be ready to drop the more confusing material and move on. Of course, players who Get It will help others who don't

You want to come away feeling good about the team's overall understanding of the material, balanced against how many items you were able to go over. Compromises of reps and time are inevitable; no practice will be perfect from that standpoint. Still, knowing that you made it pretty smoothly through three or four larger agenda items in one hour will deliver confidence to you which will translate to game-day preparedness.

Be flexible: Although you must use time efficiently, don't be a slave to your practice plan. Getting 60-minute practices "down to a science" takes constant trial and error, and revision of your "rundown." It won't always go perfectly, but when you get it right, the results often translate directly to the court. Most of your players will know where to be, and if they aren't sure, you'll know how to advise them.

Pro tip: Keep track - in a notebook or on the Notes app in your phone, etc. – of what you actually worked on, what worked and what didn't, and what you didn't have time for. It'll help you structure future practices.

**For more ideas, look at YouTube for youth basketball skills workouts and practices you can grab ideas from; and by all means, consider approaching local 1-day workout sessions for a possible team outing.

AN ACTUAL FIRST-PRACTICE AGENDA, AGES 7-8
YMCA PRACTICE #1

SHOOTAROUND/Hello - 5 mins

Hello/we're excited to coach

Teamwork: Try hard, never give up, good sports

Importance of listening

OFFENSE - 15 mins

1) Drill: Dribble relay & dribble tag

2) On Offense: If you do not have the ball, what do you need to be doing?

 -MOVE WITHOUT THE BALL -HELP / COME TO THE BALL / SPACING

 Drill: Rebound and GO!

3) Discuss fast break offense

Drill: fast break (3 guys - shoot 1 layup and run break)

DEFENSE - 15 mins

1) How to defend

Drill: defending -shuffle, hands up, up and back, side to side

2) The Lane Is Ours!

SEE THE BALL

Drill: defend lane / STOP THE BASKETBALL

3) Drill: Keep Away

LAYUP PRACTICE - 5 mins

2 teams, each race to 10 made

SCRIMMAGE WITH INBOUNDS practice - 15 mins

(Remainder of time)

AGES 7-10: A TYPICAL PRACTICE

6:55-7:00 p.m.   Arrival and warmup (shooting)

7:00-7:05   Center Circle - go over the last game, tonight's practice

7:05-7:15   Drills - 2 or 3 stations

                   Water break

7:16-7:30   Install defense — *and* install offense

- Do these at the same time
- Use half-court only
- Try hard to have minimum of 10 players (even if it means an older sibling, or a parent Stand-In)

7:30-7:35   Inbounds plays

7:35-7:50   Scrimmage (incorporating the defense, offense and inbounds plays you used)

7TH-8TH GRADE - A 2-HOUR SUMMER PRACTICE SCRIPT

AGE 13-14s — SUMMER PRACTICE #3

** HOUR ONE **

6:55 Jog 3 laps (take a ball with you for the first 2). Find a partner and an open basket... 1 shooter, 1 rebounder... shoot 10 FTs and 10 elbow jumpers - then bring it to center circle

7:05 CENTER TALK

Great job last game - finding our shots, controlling tempo
Stepping it up
Scouting report - Upcoming opponent - their approach and scouting top players

WHAT TOMORROW NIGHT'S ABOUT

Win possessions

Specifics we must improve - speed and physicality

Box out. Get hands on the ball / slap it loose when it's below anyone's shoulders. Make nothing easy... Let's not get into foul trouble, but let's also not be afraid to put them on the foul line if we need to.

Get back on defense quickly, "stop ball" — Must not give up easy transitions

DEFENSE TOMORROW

All - Our defense is why we have been so successful...

Think about what do we need to work on - what can we still improve on?

Let's get deflections - active hands

ABOVE ALL - Commit to defense: Win loose balls, BOX OUT.

Most teams never box out. Take this category because a missed shot is a second-chance opportunity

Deflections / hands / rebounds / tie-ups / dive

7:15 DEFENSIVE

1. Their offense, <u>our defense</u> versus

- Our press

Sprint 1x, water.

7:35 OFFENSIVELY a few things

2. Our offense, their defense

- Transition - looking for fast outlet into break
- The Wheel; 212; Inbounds
- Our press break
  [https://www.breakthroughbasketball.com/plays/linepressbreaker.html]

Spread it out vs a zone

Working through a double team trap or a crowded zone

 - willing to outwork - sense of urgency

Inbounds plays and offense plays: Cut like you mean it

 -Hard cuts, get separation, GET OPEN

RUN INBOUNDS PLAY

- Run the inbounds with INTENTION - shoot when open!
- ZONE UP off the other guys' inbounds play
- both teams try it 8:00ish Shoot elbow jumpers; water

HOUR TWO

ROCKET: concentrate on controlling it.

- Don't play out of control on offense.
- focus on 3-on-2 advantage - FIND THE OPEN MAN!
- Defense concentrate on stopping the ball, defending the shot, REBOUNDING

8:20 SCRIMMAGE

Begin scrimmage with Jump Ball Play

Practice our inbounds plays

Try 212 and various Give/Go

4-OUT 1-IN Motion / don't follow your own pass / screen if you can / Get the ball into the post

Have Defense run some 2-3 and some man if time permits –

PRESSURE FREE THROWS

At the end of practice, each team lines up on baseline

1 player shoots 2 foul shots

- Makes both - the other team runs
- Make 1 miss 1 - player runs
- Miss both, our entire team runs

IN YOUR INTERMEDIATE PRACTICES

When players are younger, practices are going to be more playful. As they grow and competition begins to differentiate them, running an effective practice becomes key to getting kids ready to play at their best.

- These should be crisp, fast-paced practices. Emphasize team speed, basic screening, transition offense, and especially, rebounding.

- Install your defenses first/early during team practices… or better yet, run both at same time.

- Do the dirty work. Establish to the group that a great box-out/rebound is like forcing a turnover, praise the effort made for a deflection and diving for a loose ball, or chasing after a long rebound (you can drill these).

- A guarantee I will make, if you do this: YOUR TEAM will get to every loose ball first in every game/many of the games you play, until you run into another group that is also focused on this, and a coach who also has his or her team prepared to do it quicker.

Practice matters. There's no shortcut and no substitute for practice. Everyone needs to be there: no exceptions, as you'll be installing plays. If you run into issues of availability with the venue, find (or add!) a session on a school playground. If key team member(s) repeatedly can't make it to practice, arrange the pick-up and drop-off yourself.

If you emphasize playing a rugged man-to-man, at the very least your group will generate more chances on offense, and learn by experience what it needs to overcome obstacles it may have faced such as an offensive talent gap, or a physical differential, often the case at the intermediate level.

At this age, there is little difference between practice and a game. You have to practice the same way you perform. Good luck being half-assed in practice when you have a real game to play.

THE POWER OF 3-on-3

At a later point during your season, devote most or all of a practice session to having the team members compete 3-on-3.

Playing this way is a terrific opportunity for you and the players. The court opens up, enabling you to really see and instruct; and giving each of your players more touches and the ability to "just play" — in a manner incorporating and necessitating key aspects of the team game. It's fun, too. You can stage a mini-tourney.

You'll see all of your players get instantly involved and gain immediate understanding of where they need to be and what happens if they don't get there. Going 3-on-3 lets them help over in Man, demands that they close out, enables practice of the pick-and-roll, lets them screen away, and gives them opportunities to make backdoor moves and create, with and without the ball. All along the way, you can (if you like) stop play to demonstrate specific points.

Switch to 5-on-5 after a session of running threes and you will be astonished at the flow of play. Confidence, chatter, driving, off-ball movement and playmaking soar. Players really learn the game at its essence in 3-on-3, and without having to first sit through a play demo. And it really shows up later.

CONSIDER ALSO:

- Go hard in intermediate (and older) practices, to induce effort in games.
- Set a tone of accountability here, as well; Be on time. Come to practice!
- Give out a Beast Award for hustle or great team-first play, etc.
- Practice game-ending situations and inbounds plays.
- Talk up positivity.
- At this age conditioning also becomes a factor; close every practice with sprints and foul-shots in fatigued state.

MANAGING PARENT EXPECTATIONS

Whether you brought your own full squad or will be randomly assigned individual players by the league, you'll want to set expectations with the parent group.

You want the parents on the same page with you. Be sure to let them know early on, via one of the earliest group meetings, your approach to practices (such as your policy on excused absences) and games. At the youngest ages: "We let all the kids play, and winning is secondary."

The majority of parents, glad that their child is involved in the team activities, will turn it over to you. They will have few, if any, difficult questions. However, it's the occasional parent who raises concerns about their child's role. Nine times out of ten that initial question will be some form of, "Why doesn't my child start / play more minutes?"

When it comes to their own children's abilities, parents will have a natural bias, and often aren't able to be as realistic as a coach can be. What is unique is that the coach almost always has the team's best interests in mind. Shoot straight with them and focus on what you see with the group as a whole, their child's positives, progress made, and areas for further skill development.

Listen to what they have to say. Adjust accordingly. When a parent cannot accept the feedback and remains critical, stay on message. Team comes first. Hold your ground. Oftentimes it's not personal. Years ago, when my players were very young and all of us were just starting out, our team was randomly assigned a player whose father had apparently been expecting a Mike Krzyzewski-level coaching experience. Midseason he phoned, expressing disappointment with the level of league play and my teaching, and pulled his son. He told us that the experience was too introductory, and said that he was seeking a more advanced team, and tournament play. We advised the family where they could find a more competitive experience at a suburban venue. The boy, a solid athlete but raw at basketball, would eventually develop into a good high school quarterback at a nearby school.

PLAYING UP

"Playing up" becomes a reality, as skill and competitiveness advance. Every season in the Middle School league I helped administer, parents of a few of the more skillful sixth graders asked for their child to "play up" and compete in an older age group. Thus, a handful of 12-year-olds (usually, five or fewer) would be playing with and against 13- and 14-year-olds.

One particular year, we fielded requests from parents of nine sixth graders in what is normally a 7th-8th division of around 72 players. Thus, each of nine teams would be assigned one of the younger players.

The larger number gave rise to discussion. There are advantages for both playing up (better competition, more physical play, more of a challenge) and staying in the lower division (learn to be a leader, play any/all positions, learn to be a go-to player).

It's a challenging topic, and no opinion here is incorrect. Basketball is a sport where "if you can play, you can play," so to speak. One year my sixth-grader John stayed in the 5th-6th division while his twin brother Rob requested to play up. Each chose for himself, and each enjoyed a positive experience.

In the end, our league did not restrict playing up, and in my opinion, it worked. The kids who moved up were ready to compete as role players against bigger boys. Their absence at the level below enabled "next player up" leadership opportunities for the sixth graders who stayed.

COACHING YOUR CHILD

If you have a son or daughter on your team, and it's very likely you will, you have to take extra steps to treat your child the same way you would handle every other player on the team. I can assure you every parent will track comparatively whether you allocate the same or more minutes to your child than to others; whether you single out your child often for praise, team leadership, or even criticism. My advice: put on your coaching hat, and be your child's Coach — not Mom or Dad — during those hours.

LEAVING PRACTICE - YOUR PREGAME MESSAGE TO YOUNGEST PLAYERS:

- Let's play fair, and have fun tomorrow
- Hustle!
- Get stops: Turn defense into offense
- Make good decisions on offense. Good passes, good shots
- Outwork the other team, and be positive

Here's a sample pregame message, from a 7-10 team

- Let's have fun and be good sports

- What's our offense? (Fast break) Our half court offense? (2-1-2)

- The Lane Is Ours! Everyone sag toward lane and help if/when the ball is more than one pass away from your man

- Run. Let's use our speed & ball-handling to push tempo of the game when it makes sense to

- Protect the basketball. Pass up poor options in favor of keeping possession alive

- Be hard to guard. MOVE TO GET OPEN And a sample from a 6th-grade summer team:

- Pressure their guard play. Make it hard for them to ever involve their bigs

- Turn defense into offense: Deny, deflect, disrupt

PRE-TOURNAMENT EMAIL - AGES 11-12

And finally, here's Some of what we told our kids before a lively, city-wide fifth and sixth grades tournament that we won:

What have we talked about all year?

1) "TOUGHNESS"

It's what we say whenever we break huddle. On Saturday, let's be pit bulls guarding the ball...

- Get deflections: hands in the passing lanes
- Turn defense into offense: It's what we've been doing ALL YEAR... Win those 1-on-1 loose balls, box out and win the rebounding battles

2) "DEFEND SMART"

- We call it 'defensive overplay,' and it is the "right way" to play -- all-out hustle, fearlessness, making our own good luck
- Avoid fouls by defending with our feet and not reaching in, or around
- Same goes for blocking shots, the right way -- arms are straight, going for the ball only (not the hand or arm)
- Persistence and toughness means going on, even when you'd rather take a break... Having the willpower to Hang In There for longer

3) "LOCKED IN"

- "Locked in: means we run our plays, move without the basketball!, and we communicate with one another.
- It also means: Settle in, relax… and let the other team be in a hurry.
- "Finish" your shot. (Make sure you get up a nice, good, on-target shot, then follow your shot / block out someone)
- Do everything like you mean it… when you go to fake out your man get open, make your cuts sharp
- On defense, it's "Ball U Man" - see your man, but know where the ball is, always…

  Run the inbounds play with speed and with purpose (hard cuts to get open, get the pass, shoot!)
- Block out distraction: My man is taller or faster than I am, the other team is fouling and we're not getting any calls… Doesn't matter. Play on.

4) So... "Tough," "Defend," "Lock in" ... and FINALLY — BELIEVE!

- LOVE YOUR TEAM. Coach David & I love this team's attitude! You guys are successful because you believe in each other.
- TAKE THE WIN! A famous coach once said, "You are what your record says you are." You have proven over 9 games that there is no better basketball team than this one. Let's go be the team that TAKES THE WIN.

We have gotten better every day, every week... NOW, IT'S OUR TIME. LET'S GO PLAY OUR GAME... BE THE "BEST US" WE CAN BE. Great season, guys... **See you tomorrow!**

WHO'S COMING? WHO ISN'T?

Important: ask the parents over email or text to confirm whether their child will be attending each practice and each game. This is a critical success factor and a must before you can script your rotations and lineups.

SCRIPTING THE LINEUP

Scripting a lineup takes a little time — and it is just possibly the most important thing you can do the night before a game.

If you take the time to script a lineup just once in advance, you'll see immediate advantages. A pre-printed list ensures all players are given time. But perhaps more importantly, scripting saves you valuable time and limits in-game chaos associated with rotating eight, or ten — and often more — young players.

- The night before the game I use "stickie" notes (one per player) on a clipboard, placed in two vertical rows to visualize which five players are currently on court and off.

- Each time a player gets a rotation, using pencil I make a tick mark on the stickie note. I now know "John has been in three times; I need to get Rob his third turn."

- In a given game I am substituting (or "rotating") one or two players about every 4 minutes.

- Strive to substitute a ballhandler for a ballhandler, an aggressive hustling non-shooter for another "floor diver" and so on.

First half

20:00 Hudson, John, Sam, Luke, Kade
16:00 Rob, John, Max, Tyler, Simon
12:00 Hudson, Tyler, Sam, Max, Simon
8:00 Rob, Davis, John, Luke, Kade
4:00 Hudson, Tyler, Sam, Kade, Rob [at the 5]

Second half

20:00 Hud, Davis, Luke, Kade, Simon
17:00 Rob, Tyler, Sam, Kade, Simon
14:00 Hud, Sam, Luke, Max, Simon
11:00 Rob, Tyler, Max, John, Kade
8:00 Rob, John, Luke, Max, Simon
4:00 Hudson, John, Rob, Luke, Kade

ROTATIONS AND SUBSTITUTING - YOUNGEST AGES

Figure out who your better dribblers are and when you substitute, always have at least two good ball handlers on the floor. At all times, you'll benefit from having minimum two or preferably three individuals out there who can dribble, pass, cut and move the ball around.

In addition, look to always have someone out there who can rebound and defend "in the paint." This player might not necessarily "big," especially at the younger levels.

During the game, have your assistant keep the rotations sheet and make most of the actual substitutions. This frees you from bench distraction and allows you to focus on the on-court action. Your assistant will be a big help overseeing this script, and with any adjustments to your substitution pattern, as inevitably there will be in-game changes due to matchups, injury or absence.

PRO TIP: SHUTDOWN DEFENSE - AT ANY AGE

Where you place players on D is as important as who you have on court. If you're getting torched by a good, right-handed player, park your most physical defender (or your best charge-taker) on the rightside block (as you face your defense), and your overall smartest defender/deflections specialist on the right elbow. Voila, you have taken away half of the court. (Reverse this, if the scoring player is a lefty.)

Put your less aggressive defenders on the weakside low block. At the youngest ages it's a little bit like playing left-field.

PRO TIP: SUBBING - YOUNGER TEAMS

Consider starting your least-skilled or second-least skilled player — gets the entire team energized and involved

- Signals everyone that playing time is going to be balanced

- Starting is not important at this age (see below); plus, you'll be rotating the lineups all throughout the season

Start the Second Half with what you consider to be one of your stronger — if not the strongest — lineups (Making an aggressive push in the first 2:00-4:00 of the second half is a great strategy to get separation or erase a deficit)

- If someone closed the half "hot," consider keeping that player on as you return from halftime

- (With the exception of the first 2:00 of the second half) Mix your skilled/lesser skilled players throughout first 3/4 of the game

Close the game (the final quarter, or equivalent) with your best five players on court. Often I would build in my final two rotations of the ballgame so that my two most-skilled fivesomes were on court for the final 4-6 minutes

A NOTE ABOUT STARTING

Too much emphasis is placed on who starts. In the younger age groups, it's really about who finishes. Most every team we coached (K-6), we tried hard to ensure that everyone got in. Quite often, we started one of our last two bench players. With younger teams, give every player on the roster at least one start over the course of the season.

SCRIPT: FINAL THOUGHTS

Personnel and minutes grow in significance as you move up in age groups. Thus, writing a rotation the night before / in advance becomes a key success factor.

You'll be amazed at how many coaches don't do this, only to find themselves distracted on subbing, and having to play "personnel catchup" late in games.

A final point. Can you go off-script? Of course. We learned to eye-test, adjusting for foul trouble, injury, matchups, etc.

But I'd be willing to bet that the habit of scripting helped us save time, and find the right team chemistry at the right moment, in 80% of the games we played.

PREGAME: YOU

In the hour to half-hour before you play: Arrive to the venue with your scorebook roster filled out in advance. Or ask a parent to write in your players' names and numerals into the official scorebook. Make certain everyone is listed, even known absentees, and their jersey numbers are included correctly (if applicable).

Recruit your clock/scorebook parent volunteers in advance. Don't overlook asking someone to track "hustle stats" (includes categories such as charges drawn, deflections, loose balls recovered). Your team parent can help with this. You can make their life easier by advance printing-out of the "hustle" form. Here's a free example: https://bit.ly/3RcPQtH

Find out if the game will have any format peculiarities or rules (people at the scorer's table will know, or a rules/game-format sheet will be there). Examples of format peculiarities: Only playing halves, not quarters; playing with a "running" clock, not a "stop" clock. Find out how many timeouts you will have, and whether first-half TOs carry over to the second, or are of the "use or lose" variety.

When at an away venue, walk your players around, showing them any unusual floor markings. Youth sports facilities often share basketball and volleyball space; sometimes multiple lines are laid down. You want your players to see in advance where the basketball sideline and the timeline actually are.

Take a look at the printed-out rotations with your assistant. Review substitution patterns, and any additional game-plan, strategy, etc. The assistant runs the actual subbing of players. Rotations/substitutions will vary possibly — depending on the score, foul trouble, injury/fatigue and specific situations.

PREGAME MEETING WITH THE TEAM

Oftentimes your game isn't the first one taking place that day. Your players are the likely to arrive to their designated court during the second half of the previous ballgame. As that game winds down, have the players stretch (keeping an eye on the clock). Join them there for the short chat that follows. [By the way: this is NOT the "final final" huddle before tip-off.]

Focus the players on what you worked on in practice.

Guide them through the game plan, and take time to reinforce group objectives. [Example: "Let's remember to get back on defense. Slow them down, then get hands in the passing lanes and take it away. If they do get the One Shot Only, box out hard, board and clear it, outlet and go score. Run inbounds plays sharp - remember it's like a corner kick. If you get the inbounds pass, don't dribble it, don't pass… SHOOT IT!"]

Reveal the starters, if you haven't already done so at practice. One last time go over your offense, and any defensive assignments. Open it up for questions. Then let the players get back to themselves until it's time for your team to take the court for pregame warmup.

Note: Stretching out well, 10-15 minutes before a game in a hallway or corner of the gym, is as critical as getting heart rates beating during the on-court, pregame warmups. If you neglect to have them do it, it'll take several minutes into the actual game play before they're truly revved.

WARMING UP BEFORE A GAME

Whether your team plays first on the day's schedule, last, or somewhere in between, expect to have less pregame warmup time than you would prefer.

Think: probably somewhere in the vicinity of 5-8 minutes. Sometimes it'll be less, sometimes more. It all depends on whether games at your venue that were scheduled before yours are still on schedule. The venue and your game officials usually control when you actually tip off. So be ready (if they're falling behind schedule) for them to come to both coaches and express that they will be starting early — shaving time by reducing the duration of your pre-game and possibly your halftime.

TWO DRILLS

As the team begin to arrive and have court access, have your players shoot around, briefly.

We installed two and only two warmup drills, to help get our players moving and focused, and to give our teams an "initiative-taking" mindset:

1. Deflections drill (1 ball, 7 players)

This is a high-energy "Keep Away" drill, using one ball, to

instill a deflection/interception and trapping teamwork mentality.

- 4 players on offense: 2 at the elbows and 2 on the blocks. Offensive players can throw bounce, chest or overhead pass to any offensive teammate. The offense is not allowed to move, but it can pivot.
- 3 players are on defense and are anywhere they want in the paint.

Play keep away. "Get your hands in the passing lanes!" When a ball goes astray or gets intercepted, switch the nearest defender out, and bring the last offensive player to touch it on to the defense; don't forget to rotate in your observers, too.

"If I deflect and cause the turnover, I get to go on offense; If I threw the bad pass, I move to defense."

Note: If you only have time for one warmup drill (in addition to shooting), choose this one! You'll be amazed at how it primes the defense to get hands in the passing lanes.

2. Half-Court Full Speed Layups

1 ball, 2 lines

- Line one, offense is at midcourt
- Line two, one defender — and this location is crucial — starts at the foul line. (The others in the defense waiting line should stand out of bounds underneath the basket)
- Toss the ball to the offensive player at the midcourt timeline
- The offensive player must, at full game speed, drive for

a layup - NO JUMP SHOTS and NO STOPPING ALLOWED!

- (Later in drill, you can customize some reps to allow for a jumper)

- The defensive player must wait at "foul line extended" to pick up (in other words, he can't start to apply pressure until then -and he must go at game speed also)

Anything you can do to promote attacking the basket will benefit the entire group. This particular drill gets the juices flowing and is an effective reminder to drive rather than settle for jumpers. In youth basketball, especially younger ages, perimeter shooting is not going to be where the most points originate.

"FINAL FINAL" HUDDLE

Bring it in with about 1:30 to go, less if you're a quick talker. Have the briefest of reviews of maybe one or two main points for the game, close with words of encouragement ("Have fun out there!"). Then fists up/together in the huddle. Break huddle with, "DEFENSE!" or, "GO HARD!"

Now, you're ready for tip-off.

4
GAME TIME

"Welcome to Indiana Basketball."

-COACH NORMAN DALE

IT'S TIME TO PLAY

OUR PHILOSOPHY, IN A NUTSHELL:

- Win Possessions
- Score!
- Get Back
- Stop Ball
- - REPEAT -

OFFENSE: WIN POSSESSIONS

Think of football. To score, you must first possess the ball. It's no different in basketball.

Possessions are precious. So, how do you get more of them?

Beginners — More Possessions, How?

- Defend and turn over
- Good dribbling and passing so you don't turn over
- Box out and rebound
- Tie-ups / jump balls
- Hustle

Intermediate/Advanced— Age 9 and Up

- Be stronger with the ball (use body to shield) so you don't turn it over
- Get back on D faster
- Deflections, defensive help/overplay/hustle to force turnovers
- Defensive rebound better

- Hold your position in the post, box out strong
- Take a charge
- Get out on the break faster
- Shoot earlier in possessions - but take [and make] good shots
- Offensive-rebound better

SCORE

With limited practice time together, you're going to want to keep things simple.

Your Offense is the fast break. (That's Option 1).

Preach "first shot mentality." You want the player with the first open shot at reasonable range to take that shot.

- If they pass too much at this age, they will eventually turn it over. Better to shoot it and crash the boards for second-chance buckets.

- Our teams got a lot of putbacks because we drilled rebounding and boxing out, and that included boxout on offense.

Option 2 is a simple set — not a play — that we referred to as, "2-1-2." If our guards are in more of a half court / walking the ball up situation, we had them go into a set, allowing them to make cuts, screen and move the ball. See below.

More sets, fewer plays: Loosely described, a set provides the starting point from which the players can then create.

Sets are useful for letting the players learn by experience by seeing firsthand, "What happens if I go here / try this?" Sets give natural place to be and spacing on the floor. From there, let them move and cut, and improvise.

The Fast Break, AKA "Transition" offense

At this age, the best offensive option is fastbreak off a miss/rebound. Get everyone running/involved, go for rebound if teammate misses the layup.

After the opponent misses, and you rebound, transition scoring is a golden opportunity to move up court as fast as you can and score before the defense has a chance to set up in the half court. Likewise, following a made basket by the opponent, emphasize immediately grabbing the ball, passing it in and getting all five quickly up court.

- Teams of any age can practice transitioning from a defensive rebound, into a multi-player fast break, culminating in a lay-in off the backboard
- When the opponent's shot goes up, box out first, and have the teammates closest to the sidelines, away from the goal, move into in outlet positions
- Encourage the rebounder to secure the ball, dribble in the open court and for the outlet teammates to fill lanes as they all move down the court together
- Drill in practice: Off the defensive rebound, have the rebounding player turn and look to pass it to the outlet players, who are set up higher (just inside either hashmark, e.g.) at/near sidelines

- Fast breaking is easy to install, it's fun, and it promotes the offensive basics [pass-dribble-shoot]
- Playing up-tempo from the start also will gives your players an unconscious "Go!" Factor that helps them be more active in all areas such as half-court defense

DEFINITION: A Box-Out is defined as the act of positioning yourself (after a shot goes up) between the opposing player and the basket, to rebound the ball in anticipation of a missed shot.

Bonus fun:

- Pull up on the fast break and shoot a three-pointer
- Shoot a corner jumper off of an offensive rebound

"The 2-1-2" - Your Halfcourt Offense Set

- Any time your first choice [transition offense] isn't there, have your five players head toward any of five spots in your 212.

Put the team in a simple "2-1-2" set. Two guards at the top, left and right wings in the corners, and bring your post to the free throw line: That's a 2-1-2 look, kind of like a dice "Five."

- Guards bring the ball up the floor
- Your Center is stationed at the free throw line with his back to the basket. Put him there and allow him to move from elbow to elbow, tracking the location of the ball. Keeping his eyes on the guard with the ball, this player is shading ball side at the elbow closest to the ball with his hands out (and hands UP!), ready to receive the pass.

NOTE: If I put arms out only, a defender attempting to steal the incoming pass has a great chance to intercept it; but if I put my arms out and also UP above my head, now if the defender tries for the grab his upward lunge is likely to either fail or result in a foul call.

You won't get this call if your Center merely has his hands out. Get them out — and up!

- Your Forwards [or wings] are positioned at the low blocks — and they are allowed to move all the way out to the corners. In addition, they are permitted to "cross over" one another and change places. A message in the 212 for your players:

  If I don't have the ball, I am looking for a way to help us during that possession.

  I can make cuts to get open, and to move myself and my defender away from the ball.

  I can come up and set a screen; then roll, and look for the ball.

  Dive for a loose ball, block out for rebound just as soon as the shot goes up from my teammate.

In the 2-1-2 you can generate a lot of give-and-go type action off of the foul line player (should be your best or 2nd best player). This player might also have a wide-open shot from there. I've seen it happen!

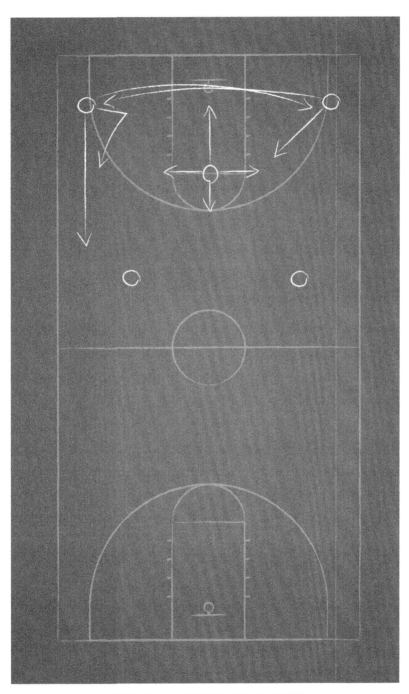

THE 2-1-2 OFFENSIVE SET

- Guards bring the ball up
- Our first look is to try to get it to our Center. Center may turn and shoot
- If it isn't there, pass to either the ball-side Forward, or to our other Guard (who has same objectives)

Guards: if I pass to the Center at the foul line, I quickly cut through the lane for a possible Give and Go lay-in

Forwards:

- If I am on the ball side when the guards arrive, I am moving up and back in my area and making cuts to leave my defender/get open for the pass

- If I am the Forward not on the ball side (i.e. I am the weakside Forward), I move over quickly to the block, looking at, and calling for, the ball; or I can get open by running the baseline to cross-over with my fellow Forward

Center:

- I am almost always at the foul line, facing the teammate with the ball, and have arms up ready to catch a pass. I'm taking care not to be in "the paint" for more than 2.9 seconds

- When I get the basketball I look to shoot, or pass it to an open player

- Often the best option is a pass back to the guard from whom I just received the ball; my next-best pass would be to the wing closest to where I am on the court

FINE TUNING: OFFENSE

Although the below tips are largely for the older age-ranges (9 and up), you might find several items, in particular #7 (Inbounds Plays), useful.

1) PROTECT THE BALL. Poor execution leads to slow starts. Any time you trail, as a group you make rushed decisions. Solve this by urging the kids to make good passes, communicate better, and make sure they're helping when a teammate's trapped/in trouble.

2) EXECUTE YOUR INBOUNDS PLAYS. This is like a corner kick in soccer. It's a set play, and a gift-wrapped opportunity to shoot and score. Often coaches and players don't take this part of the game seriously enough. Get crisp on these, get open shots, and take the easy points. You can easily improve here.

3) BE MUCH, MUCH HARDER TO GUARD. When on offense without the ball, MOVE. Screen, cut, and communicate with one another. This one's an easy fix also. Be willing to work harder on offense (and don't treat it as a chance to rest).

4) PLAY YOUR POSITION. When you fail to play your position, other players end up being in the wrong place. (e.g., guards trying to box out vs. much taller defenders underneath).

For older players who know better: If you instructed someone to switch and they repeatedly don't, pull them out of play for a brief word, and a brief rotation on the bench. Some of best coaching counsel is made to players on the bench during the game.

5) IMPROVE YOUR SHOT SELECTION. In the heat of battle, the kids can get in too much of a hurry. A bad shot is the same as a turnover. Remind them to square up, relax as they aim and release, just like in a shootaround.

6) TEMPO. Try to be the team who controls the speed and rhythm of a given game. If you are playing a group with a deliberate, slow-it-down offense, apply pressure, force a bad shot, grab the rebound and go score in transition. If you force the opposition to adjust to your game speed and rhythm, you gain advantage as a group.

7) NO, REALLY — IMPROVE YOUR INBOUNDS PLAY EFFORTS! Forcing tie-ups (with the next possession determined by the scorer's table arrow, or by the official tracking possessions) multiple times during the game is a useful and often contagious tactic of an aggressive any-age defense. Along with the many natural turnovers in a typical youth game, this will give your team numerous under-the-basket inbounds opportunities. We only ever used two inbounds plays, and both did the job:

- STACK — Use a "stack" AKA a straight line that starts at the opposite-side elbow (top corner of the foul line & the lane). The front player in the line cuts to the ball-side block. Next player to the ball-side corner (for a possible three), the third turns and screens for the fourth player. The fourth player moves to the opposite block for an easy lay-in opportunity.
- 4-HIGH — Use the easy, "4-high" set-up as mentioned. One player as inbounder, the other four start above the

three-point line (or use the foul line extended). They cut hard to get open anywhere. It's just that simple. [You could customize that, so the kids don't feel lost. Have the player nearest the inbound cut to the corner. The middle two can cross over (picture a giant "X") as they head to the blocks. The last man, from the opposite side, cuts across the top for a nice open look at the ball-side elbow.]

"4 High" as base play. Easy to teach and fun for the team to run.

- One inbounder underneath
- Four teammates free to be anywhere behind the foul line extended
- Ref hands ball to Inbounder, who then slaps ball [or says, "GO"]
- Four players cut to the ball
- Make fast cuts, recipient should try to shoot it off the catch and everyone box out

Getting Better Offensive IQ: The basic offensive "sets" give them something that clicks with them. If shots are falling, that always helps. But that may be a function of having more confidence and seeing that it's a good shot within the offense.

You'll know things are clicking when the group can move the ball around and wait patiently for the defense to offer an opening. Your wings and guards can pressure a (especially zone) defense with great passing.

But perhaps just as important to really open things up are: shot fakes and ball fakes, followed by short penetrations. These create drive and pull-up jump shot opportunities and/or assist opportunities for an open wing.

DEFENSE

They say that "defense wins championships." I'll offer a slightly different mantra: defense can keep you in nearly any game.

Teams can go cold on offense. There will be games when your team, no matter how skilled, cannot shoot straight. You can count on this happening. It WILL happen. When it does, a foundation built upon defensive effort goes a long, long way.

STOP SOMEBODY Everybody loves offense. But if you want to win and contend, first, <u>You Gotta Stop Somebody</u>. It's easy to instill a defense-first mindset, yet so few coaches appear to be interested. Seize the opportunity.

For many teams, defense is an afterthought. Of course, this is a trend as well in sports as a whole. People want to see touchdowns, home runs and three-pointers. Many basketball fans come to see high-scoring basketball games.

During our first three seasons, we realized that few other coaches were trying to defend well, so we seized that as our competitive advantage.

Year in and year out, our teams excelled at defending. (It helped that we had good scorers, as well, on some of those early teams!) We preached defensive "pressure" (which when younger, simply means maintaining form/position, intensity and awareness).

We found that if we praised deflections and hustling effort in our team defense, we got more and more of it.

Hustle, we learned, really is contagious when you reward it.

Suddenly, ten hands at a time were outstretched. Ten arms were disrupting the passing lanes. Players were diving for loose balls. Others learned how to force "held ball" tie-ups. And we discovered that when we equated "steal" with "intercept," our football- and video game-loving players became really motivated to make the big "pick."

If your teams are willing to defend — to pressure the ball at all times — appropriately, the less skillful offensive teams in your charge will be able to stay close in just about every game, regardless of your opponent's skill level.

You will want to emphasize:

- No middle penetration. When an opposition player has the basketball at the top of the key, your defenders direct that player toward the sideline. When an opposition player has the basketball on the wing, direct him toward the baseline.
- Move when the ball moves. Whenever the basketball moves, every defensive player on the court should be adjusting his positioning on the court. By keeping the importance of this in mind, players will learn that they must stay alert at all times and anticipate passes that they may be able to deflect. The difference between a

steal and an open layup or a missed steal and a breakdown of the defense can be a fraction of a second.

Want to have the best defensive unit in your league? Play tough-minded, "helping" Man defense. Here's a great resource: https://www.basketballforcoaches.com/man-to-man-defense/

STOP BALL: TURNING DEFENSE INTO OFFENSE

- Proper defensive form: knees bent, arms out facing ball
- Pressure the ball in the half-court — Intense guarding of the player who has ball. When your team understands to pressure opposing guards, you will be much harder to beat.
- See the Ball. This is crucial even for the youngest players. Also known as Ball-U-Man, these are the three things to track with your eyes at all times, when you are defending your man, away from the ball. The 'ball-you-man' stance means that the defender is pointing one hand at their opponent and one hand at the basketball. They must be able to see both with their peripheral vision at all times. Emphasize "See The Ball," and "Ball You Man!"
- "Deny one pass away" — The player from your team who is defending the nearest (most apparent) potential recipient of the ball must get up on his man, closely guarding with arm-bar to "prevent" (or disrupt) that pass option
- Five defenders always stay "ball side" — If the ball moves to the right side, your five defenders shift accordingly. They don't stay in the original facing

position, but rather drop to now be between their man and the basket (aka "lower" than their man) shading so they are closer to the ball

- Front the low post — Our lone defender who will actually move so he's in front of the offensive player closest to the goal, facing the ball but also using his backside to feel his man, and stay directly in front. When this is executed properly, you've either eliminated the pass to this player, or you've dramatically increased potential steals and deflections when the pass attempt comes

- Help over (and recover) — We emphasize (and drill) that "the lane is ours!" The rule we give our players: Anytime the basketball enters the lane, and I'm nearby (but defending another player) I can leave my man, hands up and out, to go pressure and try to disrupt the basketball… Then I must decide to quickly return to my man. I maybe will entirely leave my man, briefly, or it might look more like a "lunge over and back" to swipe as the ball goes by, before I jump back to again defend the player I am assigned to. More on this below.

- Rebound. What you emphasize, or reward, in practice you will get more of. If you praise a great practice or in-game box-out (one where the ball hits the floor, for example, before anyone else on court is able to get to it), you will see it again, and from more than just the one player.

HOW TO DEFEND AN OPPONENT BREAKAWAY

Too many teams and players concede the breakaway shot. I am here to tell you to go after that shot. Because the reality is, any young player on any "steal/interception and breakaway" is going to be feeling the "alone in the spotlight" attention, and there is as good a chance that he or she will miss the lay-in as make it.

Your job is to instill in your kids a mindset of all-out effort at all times, even in this seemingly "automatic" opponent scoring chance. Here's how:

Know the game situation: Are we up or down? Is this an urgent situation?

Teach all-out sprinting pursuit, no matter where the steal and breakaway began closer defenders, try and jam the breakaway player's angle of approach. A faster defender who's sprinting just might have a chance to knock the ball forward from behind before the shot goes up.

Just preach being aware and careful not to make contact/foul. If your defender(s) does not have a play on the ball, don't risk the personal foul and "And 1" – instruct your player to pull up before contact

All your defenders should play for the rebound off the miss... Keep track! The miss is not at all uncommon in this situation. Your kids have to buy in to hustling here, however, so that they get the rebound. When it happens, and it will, the missed breakaway that we then are able to corral becomes a huge boon to our emotional state as a group.

[A note I wrote to a coaching friend]

We have a situational thing we call "The Lane Is Ours," where in practice, we preach leaving your man — when the ball is entering the lane dribbled by any opposition player — to go stop the ball.

In practice situations, we'll shout, "THE LANE IS OURS!" and the kids then all become fiercely focused on clogging that area and ganging up on the ball.

During game play, when our players are setting up/awaiting the offense to come downcourt, we also remind them of this with: "Stop the ball, then stop your man!"

If our players see the ball advancing quickly the other way down the court (a good dribbler or a good pass), everybody tries to sprint back as fast as they can to the paint area -- We do not even really emphasize having them cover a man.

They get mindful of it during games and it's rewarding to see them remember to get back or immediately call out our battle cry and clog the lane without us having to say a word.

On D - we really work on putting pressure on the ball handler early on, and then our other players try to deny "one pass away" - and continue to deny opportunity for their man if ball is elsewhere. Often the other team's guards will throw the ball away or make some other turnover by just our applying pressure. We have 2-3 players who love relentless pressure and it just becomes infectious.

We try not to let the other team do anything uncontested. No pressing is allowed, but we will at times have one or both of our defensive guards meet their guard at the timeline.

We give out our highest verbal praise for hustle plays (like following your own shot on O), for staying with your man when he is without the ball, for forcing turnovers and playing awesome team "denial defense."

When our better scorers make a shot, we usually give a quick "fist pump" or "golf clap" -- as if we expected that success. (We of course go crazy when a more timid shooter or "defensive specialist" drains one.)

[One final thought on this one: Since there are no fouls in our league, and no stealing off the dribble is permitted (the ref treats this as a mere turnover, or same team simply gets ball out again on the side), we have learned that if the opponent intercepts and is headed other way, we have our faster defenders in open court run up BEHIND the ball handler and knock ball FORWARD / loose out of his hands — a legal play under this rule. Opponent now gets the ball out on the side, giving us time to set up our D... and best of all, that ballhandler we harassed will now be hearing footsteps.]

When you are in MAN:

- The whole point of getting UP on your man is, he now must decide to pass, shoot or drive. In addition, he is likely to pick up the dribble, and now you go for the "tie-up" and force the jump ball

- If he's a good perimeter shooter, if he is a skilled and confident handler, he'll put a move and try to go past you...

BUT HELP IS THERE - so play up on the man. Give him no chance to shoot; you pressure the pass he might be making

- and if he drives, TEAMMATE or whoever is there. He's got nothing

PLAYING ZONE

The 2-3 zone defense is the most commonly used zone defense. It has the advantage of protecting the inside, lane area, and keeps your "bigs" inside. Its weakness is it is vulnerable to good outside shooting, with open areas on the wings, point and high post. Weakness of a zone:

- Does not defend well against the three
- Gives up too many offensive rebounds
- Doesn't defend the high post
- To combat this, at times we play a highly active 2-3 we call "Beast"

BEAST: ACTIVE 2-3 ZONE

There are a couple of ways to play in the zone. One is follow the ball around with your hands up, but what we want to do is aggressively get out after the basketball and trap everything. "Beast" is all about overplay on the ball. Once the ball is passed anywhere on court, there is a rotation that sprints urgently to pressure the ball and the normally available passing spots. There needs to be a Ball Guy, a Deny Guy, and guys in Help no matter where the ball goes. Attached is a good idea of the key positions on the floor for this zone — It's all about communication, and the two at the front have to work hard to cover a lot of territory.

- Whether in the 2-3 regular, or in the 2-3 "BEAST" special overplay zones, be active in putting pressure on the basketball especially when it is out on the wing. If we can pressure guards/shooters and make them work

much harder to get to do what they want to do, they are going to feel the need to either pick up the dribble or pass to get rid of the basketball, rather than drive or shoot a jumper.
- With BEAST we are trying to force them to give us the ball in whatever way we can: via turnover, bad/contested/rushed shot, mental fatigue or mistakes caused from pressure that we are applying.

On everything we want players, not robots. We may say, "Go stand over here in this defensive look," but we also want or players active and free to make decisions.

Watch As Defensive IQ Improves: You'll find that as players become comfortable in the defense, they will start to recognize where they need to focus effort and even make adjustments themselves. Communicating like a team, you will notice them identifying who is hurting the defense most.

Take their advice. Our 11-year-olds transitioned (in-game and on their own) from a 2-3 zone to a Box-and-1, modified to prevent one skillful individual from being as comfortable as he'd been in earlier action. Our entire defense responded and we turned a halftime deficit into a win.

Weak Areas of 2-3 Zone:

LATE-GAME STRATEGY

If you have a decent lead, say six to ten points, in the final five minutes of a game, you want your team to "run clock" on offense. It at all possible, challenge your players to pass up jumpers from out, and choose higher-percentage shots such as close-in jumpers and lay-ins.

(At any time) try and avoid them chucking "NBA Three" attempts in the first few seconds of an offensive possession! Instead have your players, if they are capable, pass and cut, prolonging possessions.

On defense playing with a lead during these final few minutes, play half-court defense and tell them, "No fouls!' Emphasize for them to "defend with your feet," rather than reaching in.

If trailing late: Your offense has got to operate quickly, but still must maintain good form and play for good, open looks — nothing panicky or willy-nilly. Emphasize that while we are now in a hurry, we're also calm.

Then, apply pressure after a score. In the youngest ages, this may simply mean, have your defenders pick up at halfcourt and face guard the ball (defend the ball player hard, with your defender up on the ball to try to get a tie-up or at least force a rushed pass).

DOG: At certain times in a game, and this is one of them, we like to unveil a devastating half-court trap we call, "Dog."

- Set up in what looks like a 3-2 or 1-2-2 halfcourt (if you are not permitted to play zone, have your kids match up more or less in that look).

- The top 2 defenders close out, at full sprint with hands up, on the ball, as soon as it crosses the timeline – your wings sag then explode to look for the interception and fast-break lay-in.

DOG" - HALF-COURT TRAP

- The trap is full speed and begins as soon as the ball reaches the timeline and not before.
- Get your two fastest/scrappiest on-ball defenders. They have to play it cool/act casual until then.
- Your best rover/"safety" goes for the interception, and from there it's a breakaway or a 3-on-1 break

Trailing late, the name of the game is to prevent them from scoring and from running excessive seconds off the clock.

- Go for steals and tie-ups.
- Box out and then get the ball to our guards and run.
- If you score, you might use a timeout to talk to the group about the situation, set up a fullcourt or a trapping halfcourt press, and whether (and whom) to foul, to send to the free throw line, etc.

If the game is tied with only a few seconds to play: Usually someone will have called time.

Use the time to discuss defensive matchup. Try to have your best defender "full deny" their best player from getting the ball on inbounds — and if he does get it, apply solid pressure to force him to give up the dribble or pass it away, etc.

In a situation like a late-game inbounds play for the opponent, when you come back from a timeout, your goal is to remove the opponent's best piece from the chessboard. Have your best defender play up on their best offensive player. You are in full deny! He's not getting the basketball... and if he's the inbounder, he's not getting it back.

MISTAKES: PLAY THE NEXT PLAY

If our team can't hit a foul shot, if the ball bounces the wrong way twice off the same player's hands, if a poor or questionable call goes against us, adopt a mental "re-set phrase" for all to simply Play the Next Play.

Use a mistake ritual. Here's what we did — and it's straight out of the Positive Coaching Alliance (PCA) playbook: Flush it. Adopt a toilet-flushing hand gesture with the kids, along with the team-wide policy that, when something didn't go our way, we Flush It. And then we play the next play.

ATTITUDE

"There is little difference in people, but the little difference makes a big difference. The little difference is attitude."
   – Dave Anderson, *Intentional Mindset*

It's been said the only 'disability' in life is a bad attitude. The players who have the best mindsets tend to have what I would characterize as "constant good cheer," and teammates and coaches always value them.

These young athletes play more consistently at or near their peak and always contribute to the team. You can tell in how they warm-up. You can see it in how they act on the bench. The "optimistic, hard-working" types set an example that is often contagious to the team's daily outlook and optimism for ultimate success.

The essence is that they often are independent thinkers and at the same time are team-oriented. There is no finger pointing; they pull their weight and invite others (often just with actions) to do the same.

CONFIDENCE

- Go positive and go optimistic with your squad
- Make drills fun and put the kids in challenging and fun situations both in practices and in games
- Correct <u>actions</u>, without criticizing the <u>actor</u>
- "Know the way" — Decisive/in charge. Polite with limitless self-belief
- See (and elevate when needed) body language, attitude and energy level. Take note of the best teams' "bench mob" behavior, especially during the NCAA tournament, as a great example of positivity and encouragement
- "Late-game swagger" is a real thing: It's a quiet calm, it's knowing that you and your teammates are going to make great plays, late in a close ballgame

PRACTICE COMING OFF THE FLOOR at TIMEOUTS, HALFTIMES and HUDDLES

Yep, I said it. Apply bigger energy (selectively) in smaller situations. Whenever a timeout or quarter-end stoppage occurs, teach your group to always jog it over, heads up. They need to quickly grab water, form up with eyes on you and your assistant. Get organized at this and you'll save precious seconds during a timeout.

Halftimes, we liked taking the team to a quiet spot in the gym and having everyone seated in a semi-circle on the hardwood floor, legs extended, for optimal recovery minutes. If the halftime session is longer than 5 minutes, you can send them back out for 2 minutes of shootaround/warmup. If the halftime is any shorter than this, resting and hydrating for the entire break is usually the better way to go.

IN-GAME: THE OTHER COACH

Always greet the opposing coach and shake hands/fist bump (or otherwise acknowledge). Just as you do, the coach on the opposite sideline has the best interests of his or her squad in mind. You have each put in the work and are there to help the kids safely play a game and develop in the sport. The unspoken rule of thumb: you coach your players, and they coach theirs. Understand that the vast majority of comments they may make will be well-intentioned and aimed toward player safety/fair play from their point of view.

HANDLING IN-GAME DISAGREEMENT/DISPUTE

When the coach on the opposite sideline has something contentious to say that is directed to you, remember to focus on the action in question, and not the actor(s).

Be prepared for the occasional pointed remark to you about a player of yours playing too physically. If -you- see something you really don't like, consider saying it to the officials, only.

Let the officials deal with the issue.

There will be times (although very rare in younger age groups) where you and your counterpart are in clear disagreement about a play or a call, and you will simply need to stand firm. I have experienced other coaches behaving in the following manner:

- Yell instructions to their players while on my side of the scorer's table / violating our sideline space Remedy: Point this out. Politely refuse to tolerate encroachments like this one. At the very least it's rude; more than likely, it's passive intimidation)

- Coach his team while seated at the scorer's table (This is a clear conflict of interest and should be an ultra-rare occurrence, allowable ONLY as a last resort if no paid/parent volunteer and no other alternative in the entire facility)

- Give inappropriate comment directly to my players during Play. (Never stand for this; the other coach speaks to his players, to the officials, and to you only)

And then there's the one loss you'll never forget. To say that this particular 8th-9th summer-league group ran up the score on us would be an understatement.

I've coached in blowout wins/losses but this one was different. They were a strong, deep team and would have won this particular game without the nonsense - which included:
- full-court pressing, leading by 45

- their sideline erupted onto the floor for every basket made, as if the team had just hit a walk-off homer

- Nonstop chatter. Lots of talk, talk, talk by their players

Their coach, a collegiate athlete and new to the basketball sideline, urged on his players as they threw passes off the backboard and shot layups backwards.

We simply played the game. Against the league's policy of turning off the score after a 20-point deficit, we kept the scoreboard on - and ended up losing 73-16.

The officials did a good job. I spoke to them during a stoppage and they agreed with just about everything you'd imagine I shared with them, emphatically. The league heard about this game and issued a sportsmanship email. After thanking the commissioner, I called him with a question:

"Apart from that very well-constructed email – and thanks again for sending it - have you spoken directly to this coach? Someone from the league should, before his team provokes other teams' players, coaches, the parents and referees."

To his credit, the team in question adjusted its behavior. We met them again at the end of the summer and locked down their offense, keeping the outcome in doubt until very late.

The rematch might have been trivial for their group, but for us it was the Super Bowl.

In losing to this older team, 27-21, ours was the tougher group.

Everything we talked about in practice was implemented to perfection by our boys. We protected the ball. We outrebounded, outscrapped and unnerved an excellent team for 38 out of 40 minutes.

We heard no chatter; saw zero passes thrown off the backboard and they attempted exactly one behind-the-back pass — which was stolen for a lay-up.

CONDUCT

Conduct is another big point of emphasis. ALL people associated with your team and your league need to honor the game and <u>respect officials,</u> coaches, opposing players and fellow parents.

Set your general policy early on, regarding unacceptable parent behavior (giving their child coaching advice contrary to yours; yelling at your players, the opposing players/coaches, or the officials). While the youngest players you coach will likely play on without incident, their parents might take issue with the calls, or with one another on the sidelines.

Coaches: Take control of this, before you ever set foot on the court to play that first game. In your pre-season parents meeting, take the extra steps to educate your parents and your team about competitive, spirited play with good sportsmanship. Make the point to parents that yours is the one and only voice in the "team response" to any officiating disputes.

COACHES' CONDUCT

Let's begin with what you can control: YOURSELF. And only yourself.

Your behavior is <u>calm and poised, 100% of the time,</u> on the sideline. You are unfazed, resilient. Got it? Panic breeds panic; calm breeds calm.

Coaches, it's on us to maintain player safety, reasonable competitive behavior. Keep a cool head, keep yourself in check if it gets heated, keep it limited to the battlefield, and move forward. ALL people associated with your team (and your league, really) need to honor the game and respect officials, coaches, opposing players and fellow parents. Let parents and players know in age-appropriate fashion how it's got to be:

- Discipline your players when they misbehave/fall short of this standard. <u>The bench is a strong motivator:</u> use it!
- Good behavior is directed through coaches who know how to act
- On that note, when can a player complain to an official? My opinion: that is the coach's job, and never the player's

Player Conduct

(Again, this won't come into play until roughly ages 11-12. Younger kids will simply play on.)

Coaches must work to proactively limit/halt improper conduct such as:

- Trash talk
- Any type of on-court, excessive physicality. You know what it is: jersey pulling, shoving when the official's looking the other way, etc. When I coached, those would have been subject to an entire next-game suspension from my team
- Running up the score (which is really on you, the coach). Leaving in your key players in the name of "minutes" is not a valid excuse. Use common sense

here. If you are up by 20, late in a game, your top players should either be sitting, or passing up open shots to get others the ball. Your one responsibility, when up by a zillion, is to safely run the clock to 0:00.

HANDLING ANGER

Anger — your own, that of a player, or another person — can override anything in a youth basketball game or practice. It can outweigh the correct (mental and physical) response to a given situation and jeopardize both execution and mood.

Make a thoughtful effort to understand your group's personalities and emotional tendencies. Include yourself in this. Recognizing frustration at an early stage, and defusing it before it boils over, is part of the territory in coaching. Your approach to handling these prickly situations determines much of what comes next in the gym — atmosphere (light or heavy), resilience, and outcomes.

You cannot control other players, the officiating, injuries, absences. What you can control is how you react to them. Place responsibility on yourself, on your players and on your parents to maintain good standards on and off court. Ensure that there are consequences, appropriate ones, any time the behavior falls short.

Anger and inappropriate behavior puts an unpleasant edge on everything. You're all there for the kids; try to keep the proper perspective at all times.

Take the high road, 99.7% of the time. And think before you speak.

When your player is angry

- Sub out the player. Discuss the situation, allow for some cooling-off time. Assess your player's level of calm, then re-insert (or continue to keep the player on the bench)

When the other coach is angry

- When the other coach is combative with the officials, you need to be attentive to what's going on, what the issue is — to an extent. Stay focused on your team, and don't engage directly, unless called into discussion by the officiating crew (not by the coach)
- If he is combative with you directly: above all, keep your cool, aim to defuse the situation coolly. Whatever's on his mind does not, and should never, hijack what's on yours. Stay focused.

Angry parent(s) – Your team. Set your general policy early on, regarding unacceptable parent behaviors such as excessive yelling, or giving their child contrary instruction during games. Do not tolerate a bullying parent from your group.

- When a parent from your team is directing angry commentary to official(s) – Sooner or later, you're going to encounter someone associated with your side overreacting to the officiating in a youth game. I've had it happen to the point that it disrupted game flow, and I had to reprimand the parent in the stands. N o t g r e a t . Never tolerate this.
- If the behavior is excessive ask your parent in a clear way to knock it off, then ask the parent to leave the

venue, if you feel it necessary. Take the extra step to talk it through afterward in person, or maybe via a quick call.

- When a parent from your team is directing angry commentary to you – Apart from just a simple misunderstanding/miscommunication, the topic will almost always will be related to their child's role (and playing time) on the overall team.

Angry parents – Opposing team

- In any sort of heated situation/heat of the moment, NEVER address the players of the parents on the other team. There is nothing to be gained!

HANDLING OFFICIALS

If you'd like to skip the rest of this section, allow me to summarize: Don't get caught up in officiating! Avoid distraction and coach your team.

In youth basketball games at the youngest age range, you'll likely get only one referee. When he does not make a great call, nearly always it's due more to the limitations of the task he's trying to execute: one person reviewing ten.

(In intermediate hoops, your games will be reffed by two officials, and at high-level tournaments, sometimes by three.)

Every sport has situations where the officials are not going to have the same vantage point that you, your players or your parents, have to see an obvious violation. When that happens, and it will, you have a choice.

Choice one is say nothing and let it go. I highly recommend this option.

If, however you are compelled to engage in commentary, you can make that either a productive or a destructive dialog. It's totally up to you, and the officials will follow your lead. Being overly critical isn't going to help you.

If you see something you need to bring up, do it discreetly. Get the attention of the official without histrionics, preferably during a dead-ball situation such as during free throws, a timeout or the quarter break.

Keep a respectful tone. My recommendation is to keep it positive with something like, "Mr. Official, here's what I saw: _____. What can we do better to get that call?"

Focus on the play, not the person. Officials are human beings, and they are going to miss calls. Most refs try to be proactive and almost all will listen to reason — within reason. Always focus on the call in dispute, not on the person making the call. Check out the difference in the following two examples:

- BAD: You totally missed that push! How can you not see that!
- BETTER: Could you please watch No. 23 with the push?

- BAD: Are we ever going to get that call?
- BETTER: What did you see on that play?

NOTE: Clock and scorekeepers are officials! Some venues and leagues will provide clock/book workers. Please keep in mind these people are also officials for that game. If there are no venue- provided personnel, then it's very likely that these roles are to be filled by volunteers — a parent from your team volunteering to run the clock, or a parent from the other side who has agreed to keep the scorebook. During the game, they become part of the officiating crew.

If you (or one of your parents) agree to perform one of these score table roles, remember you must refrain from inappropriate cheering or jeering of a team (or an official!).

Do not volunteer if you know you aren't capable of maintaining some neutrality or it may result in your removal from the table.

- Clock/score people – (reasonable) cheering for team is OK; criticism of officiating is NOT ok at any time... YOU are a game official!
- Clock/score duo must be working/talking together, and in agreement on running score, fouls, etc. If you and your tablemate aren't in agreement, disaster may strike. I was present once where book and scoreboard, in disagreement on the game score, resulted in the team who'd 'won' in regulation, losing in OT — all because the clock and the scorebook volunteers were not communicating during play
- Identify those parents who are competent, experienced volunteers. No parent staring at a device screen or participating in a cellphone call at the scorer's table should ever be manning the clock!

TECHNICALS - YOU

In 15 years, I received one technical foul. In a tight 9th-grade game we were losing, an official blew an obvious, easy call because his eyes were averted. I exploded, earning myself the T, even though he was the one in the wrong.

How I was able to avoid being "T-ed up" that long? Never shy when I felt the need to express a difference of opinion, I treated officials respectfully nearly always. In instances where I felt the need to speak, I asked the official a question during a dead ball, or simply pointed out what I was seeing during live play.

If you receive a technical foul: Step one, calm yourself. It isn't the end of the world. Turn or walk to your bench and regain composure. Remember the kids under your charge, re-set, and move forward. Let the team know later that you didn't agree, and you were wrong in the way you went about disagreeing. You can maintain your opinion that the call was bad, etc. After the game, if you like, seek out the official for a brief word.

TECHNICALS - YOUR PLAYER

When we were kids, drawing a technical foul as a player was nearly unheard of. It was the kind of thing that happened maybe once or twice in an entire season. (Back then, it could wreck outcomes and reputations!) If you got tech-ed you were sent to the bench, immediately, for the rest of the game. And you were definitely going to be running, all next practice.

Well, not so much anymore. This is a disturbing trend, an epidemic really starting at around Middle-School age range.

No player in the games we coached was ever the recipient of a technical foul. We had a strict, "Do not talk to the ref" rule. If a player didn't like something or was upset, he was to tell us first, and we would handle the referee discussion. Our secret weapon was the "No talk" rule, and the threat of the bench/running.

Refuse to tolerate this behavior and it will disappear.

LOSING, AND WINNING

Don't forget that coaching can be hard. You go in with high expectations but don't have control over the outcome. Playing the game the right way, with sportsmanship and respect for the opponent, is commendable.

And you should also want to win. But it won't always happen; sometimes the wins may come few and far between, if at all.

Losing is part of competition, part of life. The tough loss lingers in memory far longer than the close win. Without these hard lessons, however, we would never experience growth and maturity. Losing tests our fortitude; adversity shows us who we are. And where we are.

When you win, win with dignity and acknowledge the other team's effort – both with the postgame handshake line, and when addressing your players in the postgame. Always try to win and lose the same way, never too high after a win, never too low after a loss.

When you lose, point out the positives. What did we do well? How does this game compare to the last? What team concepts (defense, hustle, ball movement, shot selection) did we embrace? And which still need work?

When you are getting blown out (and you will, even with a talented bunch. Sometimes it just happens), ask your players to put aside the scoreboard and play the game as best they can. You all have a choice: feel sorry for yourselves, or keep working — and remember what this experience felt like.

As their coach, you are accountable. Things that went wrong for the group can be singled out, if you also take the time to offer encouragement and impending solutions (e.g., "We'll work on rebounding next practice — It'll get better!") Go look at the line and box scores for clues like TO and foul differentials. Having dismal second quarters? It's probably how you're managing your rotations/personnel.

Be optimistic and positive… It's about willingness to outwork the other team and commitment to hustle for one another. Nothing is as sweet as a win you have to work for. It will come!

For a winning season, recap both team and individual achievements. Handle a losing season the same way, focusing on overall improvement. Longer term, the key is to maintain a resilience mindset. Failure is never permanent.

(See the item just ahead, "What We Told Our 7th-graders After a 1-Win Season.")

After all, winning isn't just scoring more points than the opponent. Winning is about the group knowing how to succeed. It is about striving to play as well as possible. If the group prepares well, if it focuses on the task at hand, and if the collective attitude stays positive, maybe we win the game. Together we have improved our chances of success.

THE RIDE HOME

This one's more parent- than coach-directed, yet most every one of us who coaches is also a league parent.

Each year of the north Austin league I helped run, the Positive Coaching Alliance (PCA) would send a speaker during the pre-season to address our parent-volunteer coaches.

One of the greatest lines I've heard, and one that will stay with me always, came from this PCA gentleman's presentation regarding the parent role in youth sports, and the unintended pressures we all place on our kids.

I'll paraphrase:

> During the ride home, here's what to say regarding the game to your child/player — in its entirety:
>
> **"I love to watch you play."**

A WORD ON TOUGHNESS

"Mental toughness is many things and rather difficult to explain. Its qualities are sacrifice and self-denial. Also, most importantly, it is combined with a perfectly disciplined will that refuses to give in. It's a state of mind — you could call it character in action."

— Vince Lombardi

The routine work undertaken together by any team is vital to the group's being ready to compete and succeed. Intensity, positivity and awareness help determine how good a team can become. And you can do it without a grim seriousness even if the team's still looking for Win #1. Begin with Toughness!

What is always there for us, every night?

- D, hustle, positivity, trust
- Cutting hard and moving when you do not have the ball
- Confidence, playing the right way

All it takes is leadership and effort

- Trust in each other. Keep going
- Be positive, give it your all

When you compete, act like a competitor

- When we talk about Body Language – in hoops or in life – we are really talking about signaling to the world that we have confidence. Our body language during competition should never express anything other than focused determination.
- Toughness and swagger — Confident, not cocky. Unfazed, especially late in games, and when fatigued

TOUGHNESS: A SKILL ANYONE CAN LEARN

- Playing with Intensity is a habit... just like coasting through a game is. It's a choice, and it's *your* choice.
- Toughness comes through focus on aspects like: Winning 50/50 balls, drawing charges, playing the zone aggressively (not standing in an area), and playing through contact. Elevating your defense, hustle and urgency when the situation demands it.
- Disrupt, deflect, block, rebound, run and go score. Foul if you must - but go for the ball first.

We asked various teams of ours over the years to describe Toughness. Here are some of the most common responses:

- Serious about defense
- Trapping
- Steals
- Filling lanes
- "Finish strong"
- The ball moves, no "too much dribble"
- Knock down our foul shots
- BOX OUT
- Prevent them from getting good shots
- Work through screens
- Talk it up out there
- "Speed kills"
- Push myself when I'm tired to keep going
- Consistent and relentless

Toughness means, we sprint back if we get beat in the press. We never give up on a play going away from us and start walking. What if they miss the bunny lay-in? It happens at least once (often more) per game.

Jay Bilas of ESPN literally wrote the book on Toughness, and his creation began as commentary, then as an essay that elicited such a terrific response that a book-length exploration had to follow. I highly recommend reading.

Toughness to me incorporates focus, accountability and handling pressure. As defined, toughness is doing - without hesitation - exactly what needs to be done, the moment it needs doing, every time.

A big part of toughness in youth basketball, is "Next Play" mentality. That means letting go of a mistake or a missed shot, right away. Simply, we say "next play!" when one of our players is visibly hanging on to a negative outcome. It could be a turnover, a miss, a missed assignment or a big play for the opposition.

A huge part of team toughness is communication. In a generally good moment or a bad one; when we need to communicate details about who goes where in a set; or when somebody needs support or a sharp reminder to get it in gear — any time you have a team talking to one another on the floor, it's like you have an extra player out there.

Responding positively in pressure situations comes with conditioning the team that it's 100% normal to goof up, or to be unhappy in the moment. The key is that the moment ends, and the next one begins immediately. Flush it and move on to the next.

We talk about toughness often with our players. All youth players bring with them a different set of assumptions on the topic, and some have never even thought about it before.

Toughness and imposing your will while on the court are NOT taboo topics.

We have (sometimes) tracked hustle stats placing a high value on steals, pass deflections, jump balls, offensive rebounds, winning 50-50 balls ("loose" balls), and offensive charges. We also make a point to praise effort in areas that don't often get singled out for praise including:

- Applying defensive pressure
- Making a smart pass
- Wisdom in shot selection
- Taking care of the basketball
- Setting a good screen, or fighting through a screen

To make an excuse is to transfer responsibility. Accepting responsibility (vs. blaming others) is a choice and reveals maturity. Some players are more ready to do that than others.

Some of our advanced players will seek out additional training opportunities that directly enhance mental toughness. Typically, these are single-session basketball training opportunities, boot camps or dedicated multi-day camp that may include: weight training, sand running, working with a medicine ball, martial arts concepts and even boxing.

It's not for everyone, but the extra doses of endurance also aren't something to be automatically opposed to. Why? The workouts and concepts empower, challenge and deliver obvious focus, self-confidence and other intangibles that these youngsters might not otherwise acquire. Typically, the kids I've coached who've participated in these types of outside training activities ate it up and asked for seconds.

WHAT WE TOLD OUR 7TH GRADERS AFTER A 1-WIN SEASON

Bulls!
Coach and I are extremely proud of you guys. In tonight's 43-40 elimination loss to the Celtics, you played your best basketball of the season.

Wow, I really thought either/both of those final 3-point tries by James & Ben looked golden, and that we were headed into OT...

Some quick game numbers:
Down 18-7 early, we turned it on to cut the deficit to one at the half, 21-20. In the second, we trailed by 10 as late as 2:50 before rallying to tie the score at 40.

- For the game, we shot 17-of-57 from the field (season-highs in both FGs, and attempts); We turned it over a season-low 7 times.

Hayden had 19 points on 9-of-16 shooting, a free throw, and he pulled down 14 of our 28 rebounds. That, my friends, is an emphatic DOUBLE-DOUBLE!

- Also tonight: James contributed 10 points, including 2 threes; Ben added 5 points, 4 rebounds and 4 steals. Asa had 4 points, and Jack 2.

Season:
Despite the lone win, our improvement over the season (particularly our January-February play) is what you should focus on for next year. We rose from dead-last in offense to third-best...

- Our average game result improved from 44-28 loss to 37-35. And our defensive PPG was the league's second-best. Awesome job, guys.

Every person on this team has made big strides since we started. That goes for the "since the beginning" guys (Max,

Jackson, Abraham, Oliver, Nick, AJ, & Ben), and the "summer-league ballers" we're proud to call our newest teammates (James, Asa, Jack, Hayden and Diego).

Thanks to all the great parents who made this season fun and easy... Special thanks to all who've been hustled into scorekeeping, clock operation, video duty, snacks, first-aid, legal counsel, etc.

Championship game (teams TBD) — SATURDAY FEB 16, 3:30 pm, NW Rec Center
-We are making plans to head over and watch this game. Please join us!

104

5
MIDDLE SCHOOL

"Believe you can and you're halfway there."

-TEDDY ROOSEVELT

MIDDLE SCHOOL COACHING

Dear Reader: Eventually you and your players are going to 'graduate' to the middle-school grade levels (also, you may choose to play up as a group). Although the following aims more toward those older age ranges, there's plenty of information contained here that you can apply right now.

Coaches new to this age range will want to know what they can expect to make a smooth transition from younger age divisions.

Compared to 5th/6th age range and what came before, the Middle School [6th]/7th-8th boys age group is a different animal.

- Competition increases
- Game formats mimic school play – four periods with a stop-clock, etc.
- Expect a healthy amount of contact, and fewer foul calls
- You'll need a good press break, as fullcourt press becomes more common

Important: between the seventh and eighth grade years, strength and stamina begin to really differentiate in ways you'll easily see on the court.

MIDDLE SCHOOL: THE BIGGEST DIFFERENCES

Your goal is simple: Be ready for Middle School's bigger/older players, as well as a marked rise in the intensity level.

Starting today, it's time to get serious about:

- Defense — Deflections, rebounds, steals, hustle plays, increases in fouling. You have to defend harder and work harder on proper technique
- Tempo — Speed kills, so exploit your team speed and talent here. Show up in sound cardio/physical shape (players at this level should be jogging or running on their own), play uptempo (but smart), and with an increased sense of "smart urgency." Insert running drills to ensure your roster is fit so that the group can run, fill lanes and finish
- Shooting & ball handling — At this level, shooting skill must improve; place larger emphasis on team shooting, and on hitting free throws... If you're in close games and can raise your FG and FT percentage even by a reasonable 10%, you can win, or be right in, tight games
- Get out & practice more elbow and mid-range jumpers (just outside the paint). In particular, really emphasize and practice free throws. (Do FT team drills where all the players run if our shooter misses the pressure foul shot, etc.) Good shooters at this stage maintain their shooting form, even when fatigued
- Work on transition more: Pass, dribble, shoot and catch in transition. Passing lanes and taking good fast-break angles matter more now
- Make it about team, make it fun — Be bold, own the gym. Win every game you are "supposed to" win, and be an extremely tough out for everybody else

- Work & focus — Results require effort. You may not win every game, but no one will work harder/play smarter than your team will
- Maintain effort. Technique has to be more solid, especially when players are tired. You get better in these moments

Messages to your Middle School players:

- Finish plays. Dive. Screen, then roll. Follow your shot. Box out. Practice foul shots
- Take responsibility. When things go well, and also when they don't. That's how we learn. We expect you to turn it over, to miss shots. But we also anticipate that you will increase making good basketball decisions over time. Own it, and good things will happen

MIDDLE SCHOOL: OTHER CONSIDERATIONS

PRACTICES: Emphasize team speed, screening, transition, rebounding. Nobody coaches rebounds/boxing out, so this is a huge category ripe for the taking.

-Try to get ten people there every time during your practice session. Many youth teams may have only an eight- or nine-player roster, but you can have siblings/coaches stand in so you can run full plays and press/break etc.

- Close the game with your best five players on the floor. Most people get hung up on "who starts" but in this age range, script the endgame rotations more closely than the beginning

- Drill the team in practice on pressing, beating press and fast breaking

- Defense: Prep them to play Man, but also focus on active 2-3 zone (with ball pressure), and at minimum a basic Man press

Games - Stopclock means you'll feel a difference in how teams/coaches manage time, timeouts, substitutions and strategy

- Play all your people. While playing time is no longer "all equal" for all eight, the balance still needs to be there, 60/40ish. Most coaches have a system to get key players' rotations in at key times of the game. While no system is perfect, you do need to be mindful/shoot for solid rotations for all. Paying parents will be watching you on this. [Another strategy: if you're in a multi-game event, schedule more time for your bench players — possibly starting one or more — for a game versus a less strong opponent.]

OFFENSE

If you have the players who can adopt a running mindset (sometimes you will, sometimes you won't) then the overall best and simplest approach to your whole offense is:

- Board + Outlet Pass + Fast Break. Practice the "Get It and Go" approach

In halfcourt offense, we used a "Wheel" play (and similar "Against the Zone" overloads) as our base offensive set. Reason: easy to install/remember, kids can create from there

- Can teach a hi-lo play too. Post player flashes, then can kick or drive, etc.
- Have a "versus Man" play or plays - We ran a 5-out. If your group can perform a simple 5-out play aggressively and rotating well, it should be easy to get people open/get good open looks, and drives

Both offenses (WHEEL and 2-1-2) are easy to remember for anyone on the team, in any slot.

DEFENSE

In the halfcourt, you will quite often face nothing but zone D. Play some Man, but also run the "beast" 2-3 Overplay / highly active zone*. This is a great differentiator when run well.

2-3 ZONE we call "BEAST". Compared to regular 2-3 zone, it's more of a "rotation" using a Ball Guy, a Deny Guy, and guys in Help.

* - Beast is an "overplay," on-the-ball zone. The top two defenders have a lot more work than the bottom three do, but basically you have a BALL guy, a DENY guy. Once the ball is passed anywhere on the court there has to be a rotation. Ball, deny, and weak (Back)side lane HELP no matter where ball is and there should never be two people in same spot [SEE Chapter 4 on BEAST]

PRESSING

THE DIAMOND PRESS

Many teams run the Diamond (1-2-1-1) full court press on a made basket and fall back into a 1-3-1 half court trapping defense. It is a constant pressure/double teaming on the ball to create turnovers that result in layups. It can be particularly effective in a Rec league because most teams will not know how to beat it and will have only one or two good ballhandlers on the court at once.

Once the ball ends up in the hands of a less-skillful ballhandler hands it will likely result in a turnover.

Note: many times, teams who emphasize the press are not creative in half-court offense. They rely heavily on their pressing D to turn you over, score easy points and win games.

Break their press and make them play half-court defense.

Although it takes practice/preparation against a good press to get your team there - you'll flip the script on them in a hurry.

Here's a look at one of our Diamond press setups:

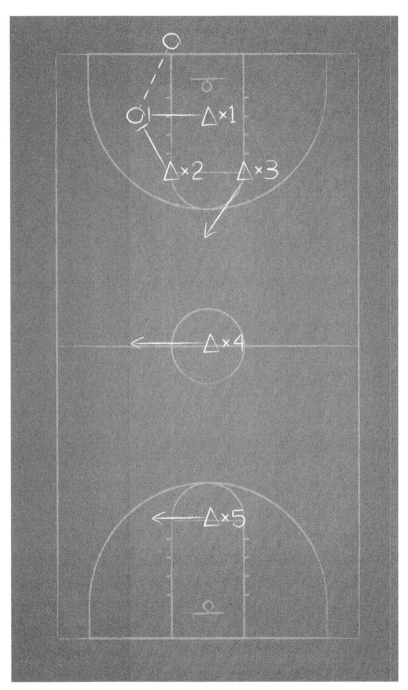

THE DIAMOND FULL-COURT PRESS

X1 Mitch forces the ball to one side but allows the inbounds pass, then attacks the player who gets the pass.

X2 Rylan cuts off the sideline, forces the dribble turn.

IMPORTANT: X2 cannot allow a pass to get behind him or over his head - if this happens you have to blast full speed down the middle of the court.

X3 John same as above, drops back. If ball is reversed, he performs same as X2.

X4 Rob is at half court and mirrors the ball.

IF THE OFFENSE IS HEADED UP SIDELINE, X4 HAS TO CUTOFF THE SIDELINE!!

x5 Patrick - back foul line, cheat to the ball side.

BEATING A DIAMOND PRESS

To beat the Diamond press: Inbound the ball to either side/corner and as the point defender is coming to set the first double team. Immediately get the ball back to the inbounder — bounce pass often works best here — and swing the opposite way.

The weak side help on the diamond can't cover both the inbounder and the other weakside guard. Have the two post players (your 4 and 5) at opposite sides at half court and have one of them (usually the opposite-side man) flash in for quick pass and then he gets it back to guards who are streaking by. Again, as with 1-3-1 fast ball movement so the double teams can't set up and NO floater/ "lollipop" passes — have to be quick and crisp)

MAN PRESS — The easiest press to teach because you're simply picking up your man, or matching up with the player closest to you.

1. Pressure the ballhandler HARD, make him give it up. This calls for the right person to defend the primary ball handler <u>without fouling</u>.

2. All other defenders go FULL DENY of the pass to their man.

Often, you will get the interception / pass out of bounds. Failing the TO, you'll often get them in chaos leading to a rushed/bad shot or possible later miscue

- But as a group, you must be fully committed to "harassment" to succeed with the Man Press, otherwise it'll likely result in an easy lay-up

PRESSURE WHEN THEY SUB OUT: Here's an advanced move that I am pinching from a coaching buddy. It's a fairly devastating idea that works, and I saw it in person during 2021 (The approximate Level is Middle School and up): When the other team subs out their point guard, immediately PRESS (it can just be a Man press, to simply pick up the nearest opposing player). Have a hand signal or a one-word signal to let everyone know. Instant turnover!

ABOUT TEACHING PRESS: I saw a stat recently that every time the Texas Longhorns pressed and successfully prevented the opponent from going "Middle," their presses generated turnovers 46% of the time.

So how would this college strategy translate, when teaching a press to the younger players?

In every press, there is a Ball side and a Weak side.

Ball side – On the ball side, your players are trapping using either a double-team, a single defender who is also using the sideline as a barrier, or all of the above. Your instruction to the ball-side people will be easy to understand here.

Weak side – When giving the players info re the weak side, what you need to stress is the *intention* — the good, smart reactive coverage & the denial away.

Those on the weak side are not statues, simply because the ball is momentarily not in their area of the court. Your weak-side young guys are the key to a successful press, but you must impart the importance of their role in that instant. Tell them the "why" of what they are doing in the press and show them how they should be reacting — shifting based on the location of the ball, anticipating a rushed or desperation pass out of the trap toward their area assignment in the press.

A SAMPLE MIDDLE SCHOOL GAMEPLAN

Our goal is to "win every possession" (score when we have the ball; get a stop on the defensive end). We want to dominate on offense and "smart gamble" on defense

- Do the little things well — Box out. Get out quickly on the fast break. GET BACK FAST on defense.

- Run. Let's use our speed & ball-handling to push tempo of the game when it makes sense to.

- Protect the basketball. Pass up poor options in favor of keeping possession alive. Inbounds passers, DO NOT PANIC. after made basket you can run baseline, use the full :05

- Be hard to guard. MOVE TO GET OPEN... Screen, cut hard, and communicate.

- GOOD THINGS HAPPEN WHEN YOU DRIVE TO THE BASKET. You will score, make a great pass to an open man, get fouled and shoot 2, hit an easy basket, or get and And-1 opportunity. And, even if you have to pass or pull up, driving adds a big threat to the defense.

- Hit our foul shots. We anticipate having to protect the lead late... They will foul; We'll relax, focus, and convert.

A TALL ORDER WE FACED (AGE 13)

What is the optimal way to defend a taller, larger team/opponent? Our 13-year-olds had to face a very LONG group of well-coached 14-year-olds who were well-coached to pound the ball down low to their post players.

Any time you are playing a plainly "better" opponent, you

must take an aggressive approach. You can't flinch or be intimidated. (I have seen games lost during pregame warmups, because the undermanned team saw the opponent and stopped believing. Never permit this to happen! See: OVERTIME)

We decided to be as physical as we could, without displacing the opponent. We played zone, clogging the lane and harassing intended pass recipients.

We achieved this by essentially double-teaming one or the other of the two opposing post players when the ball came in to either. Shifting as a UNIT successfully also turned out to be the key (we practiced this, keeping a tightly packed look with active hands), as their offensive ball movement otherwise would have hurt us.

If they'd had a shooter on the roster they would have destroyed us, because we left open the perimeter, focusing instead on the bigs and daring them to shoot the ball from deep.

After trailing by as many as 15, we were able to cut it to 3 with about 1:30 remaining. We lost by 5 in a game where we were giving up several inches at every position.

WHAT WE TOLD OUR PLAYERS BEFORE THE GAME

- Be annoying with arms out/up & bring strong defensive energy (without committing a foul)... Steal & deflect whenever your man puts ball on the floor.
- Stay as close as you can to your man and hold your position on the floor.
- Avoid reaching in... GUARD WITH YOUR FEET, NOT w/YOUR HANDS.
- Be in position for the rebound and box out — use your legs and backside to keep him behind you.
- Beat him to the spot or to the ball with your speed. He's slow... you aren't!
- Be scrappy, get tough, be ready for some contact... Our average-sized players are probably going to get elbowed, since the height mismatch puts your face right at their chest!

...AND WHAT WE TOLD THEM AFTERWARD

"You demonstrated resilience and <u>toughness</u> — outworking and outhustling them in the second half. That was one serious comeback (shorthanded, too)... You guys were dead tired but you still found a way.

- Aggressive defense, being in position for rebounds, pushing tempo on offense.

- They were definitely frustrated by our defense. Coach and I are proud of you guys for this!"

That rec team was remarkable. Although they didn't win often vs. the older lineups, they allowed the fewest points throughout the season, and took the top team into overtime. Out of those ten seventh graders, seven made school teams, and five were named starters.

MIDDLE SCHOOL: ROTATIONS AND FOULS

If you have more than eight players let your assistant oversee the "live" subbing. You and the assistant can accomplish this in any number of ways. As mentioned, I like to script the substitutions at regular, four-minute intervals. Then use that printout as a starting point for the actual player substitutions.

Reality will intervene with your scripting at the actual game. (You'll still have the "blueprint" in your pocket.) Perhaps a certain matchup is not in your favor, and you need to make a switch. Or one of your players gets in a SERIOUS groove so you elect to leave him in, when he was originally scheduled to come out. Fouls, injuries and fatigue are going to be factors, too.

Subbing a deep team: If you have the luxury of a deep roster, with up to nine good players, make the most of it. Set up a constant rotation pattern and play them all. Every 2-3 minutes someone new comes in, and the player coming out knows he'll be right back. Again, take the time to script the endgame the night before. It's good to have a reference point for whom you'd like to have out there in the closing minutes.

A note about personal fouls (5-fouls format): I am old-school with the belief that if a player receives his second personal foul at any point in the first half, he should come out for the rest of the half.

(IMPORTANT: Know who's in foul trouble! If you find it difficult to keep track of, have your assistant make sure to tell you when anyone gets to a second personal before the half; or reaches three/four fouls "too soon." It's on you as head coach to get this right. During tourney play, I would also consider asking one of your spectator-parents who's good at it to keep a scorebook, possibly seated on the bench with the team. Don't allow the scorer's table volunteers to make an assumption that you know to be a scoring error, without having the ability to dispute it. It happens!)

If he gets his third personal before the half, now his next foul — which could come in the early minutes after halftime — is a "lock" substitution for you to preserve him for later action. The time to sit a foul-troubled player is earlier, not later. (Note: a few tournaments out there have moved to an experimental, 6-personals format)

True story: One of my sons participated in a game in which his team had to play shorthanded, with only four players at the venue. They won, 56-46. All the other coach had to do was realize that he could press (even man-to-man), or simply pick up at halfcourt and just keep running fresh troops at them, to wear them down. He never did. The shorthanded squad led by as many as 18. The full team was able to cut the deficit to seven at the closest point.

It is rare when this happens, and even more rare to come away with a win. (During the 2017-18 NCAA season, Alabama's entire bench was ejected after a fight in a game against Minnesota at the Barclays Center. The Crimson Tide ended the game with only three eligible players. Minnesota won, 89-84, despite having been outscored 32-26 while being up a player, and later up two players, when a Bama competitor fouled out).

- If you're shorthanded and elect to play the game, try a 2-2 zone on defense, and get out and run in transition. Shoot threes, if your crew is able

- If you're the full-squad opponent, you have five and a bench to their four total... Turn up the defensive pressure on the short-handed group, and substitute often

NUMBERS GAME

At around this level, coaching strategy becomes more of a numbers game. If you average 40 shots per game against a good opponent the new goal is, try to get to 50 shots. Accomplishing this means that your team must get a few more stops, and score on a few more of those ten hypothetical added chances.

Create your own luck. To squeeze a single possession here or there, you have to throw different D looks (halfcourt trap; switch from zone to M2M; come out of a timeout in a fullcourt man press). Teams can no longer afford to stand around in one defense all game long.

Also, you need to get to a tighter, seven- or eight-player rotation, trusting your back-bench role players and getting them in situationally — still. You can still play every player, just be judicious.

TIMEOUTS

The following applies more for ages 9 and up (and for the more competitive youth teams), and less for the younger ages and rec teams, who are learning the game and having fun… When the younger kids need a clear break, spend that timeout without hesitation!

Otherwise…

<u>Timeouts are like gold</u>. In games you expect will be close, if at all possible, save your timeouts for when you may need to stop the clock and draw up a play in a key strategic moment. Know when to hoard them and when to spend:

WHEN TO CALL TIME OUT

- To halt the opposing team's momentum
- To give fatigued players a break
- To get on the same page before an important moment in the game
- To change your strategy
- Situationally, when a player is trapped / about to get tied up

If you use a clipboard/dry erase court diagram, have it ready. Players should grab water bottles and quickly huddle, with all eyes on you. You want to keep it simple in the huddle. Limit to one important new idea or strategy.

Note: Never spend a time-out to instruct just one player... Better to sub him out of the game, talk through the explanation quickly on the bench, then get him back in.

USING FIRST-HALF AND "USE-OR-LOSE" TIMEOUTS

In a scenario where you are allowed (e.g.) two timeouts per half, but first-half TOs do not carry over, you have the option to stop time twice during the first half regardless of situation, or forever "hold your peace" and kiss those stoppages goodbye.

If you're trying to slow the game down, or if you're trailing and simply need to break the opponent's momentum, definitely spend those timeouts. There's no point in saving them for later if you're already down by double digits. However, if it's normal gameplay, consider:

- Get a re-set timeout sometime toward the end of the first quarter (or if playing halves, near what would be the end of the first quarter. This gives everyone their first real break and lets the troops share with you things they are noticing. You can adjust accordingly. It's coming out this break when you might unveil a different defensive look, such as a press).

- In instances where it's getting late in the half, and you still possess at least one "use or lose" first-half Time Out, consider getting aggressive at the end of the half. Call time, sub in one or more players, try to "score and press" out of that timeout.

The end of the half (and first few minutes of the second half) is traditionally overlooked as junk time. Nothing could be further from the truth! In point of fact, these are great times to attack and get a little scoreboard separation.

WHY SAVE 'EM, AGAIN?

Late in a tight game, if you have your timeouts in your pocket you can slow the clock down to virtual "Matrix" time. And you give your players a valuable mental/physical re-set, some cold water, and a fast strategy discussion.

Holding for one: If your team comes up with possession of the basketball with less than :30 remaining in a half, hold for one shot with no timeout — or if you feel like they need it, spend the timeout and give the kids a quick final-play idea.

Depends on the game situation, but: You must have a group confident and capable to wait for "Go" with around 7 seconds remaining.

Not every group will be able to muster this patience; I find holding [long enough] for one to be one the hardest things for any-age youth team. Any longer than 0:30 remaining, I would just live-play.

"FREE" TIMEOUTS

During a game there are only a few opportunities where you will actually have a chance for a long break or a quick word with your team — without first having to "buy" the timeout. Some may seem obvious, others may not:

- When the opposing coach calls a timeout — late in a close ballgame, you can count on this happening
- The end of each quarter
- Any administrative stoppage by the refs (example: checking the clock/scorebook) – This will be brief, but you can still use the stoppage to convey information to your players if need be

FOUL SHOTS (BRIEF STOPPAGE): Any two-shot foul that sends a player to the line offers dead time of around 25-50 seconds; call one or more of your players over for a quick word. Keep in mind that technically they must stay on the court. Don't let them cross over the sideline to your bench.

NOT QUITE A TIMEOUT, BUT USEFUL: Subbing player(s) on every dead ball is another way, late in a close game, to send word into the ballgame with the incoming player. This strategy also gives fatigued players who are already on the floor a few extra seconds to re-set and recover. This is also a strategy that can slow a fast-playing opponent, or "freeze" for a bit longer an opposition player who is about to attempt a free throw.

6
PLAYS

"Positioning, anticipation, and technique create quickness; therefore, you can always get quicker"

-DON MEYER

KEEP A NOTEBOOK

I kept a notebook of my practices, including plays, that helped me through most all of the seasons I coached. With it I was able to track where we were, and what we still needed to work on. I printed important plays, posting them in the front of the binder. On at least two occasions, the notebook yielded ideas that helped us prevail. Following are the most-often used plays from that notebook:

JUMP BALL

Our center Rob plans to tap it to one of the two wing teammates, in this case Patrick. As soon as the jump ball is touched, Theo breaks deep, is wide open for a football pass from Patrick and an easy lay-in attempt. Also on this play, Mitch runs to ball side wing, for a possible three try, and Jack and Rob are our safeties, trailing the play in case we turn it over.

THE WHEEL

Easy to teach/easy for the kids to use as a base offense against a zone, and then create from there.

- Be hard to guard. MOVE TO GET OPEN... Screen, cut hard, and communicate.

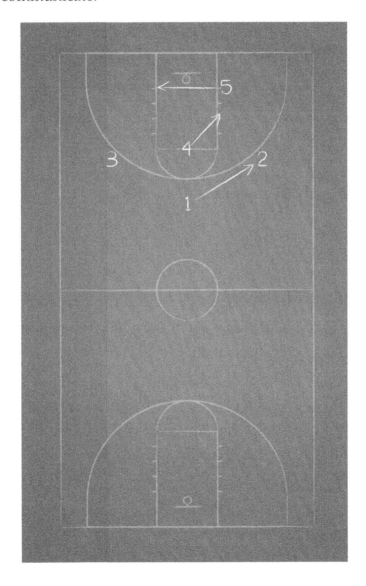

THE WHEEL - Use this as a base, give kids general rules and then let them simply play a few possessions in a row - you can tweak the set any way you like. Basics:

- Point Guard can pass it either direction. 4 has to go ballside every time. 5 goes opposite of the ball, so sometimes 5 does not move/stays right where he began.

In the example above:

a) 1 passes to 2, 4 cuts ball side and 2 tries to hit him with a pass; 5 moves to the opposite block looking to rebound.

b) After passing it, 2 can either cut through lane, or stay at elbow prepared to shoot if passed to

c) 1 cuts to the ballside corner, 3 replaces 1.

AGAINST 1-3-1

DEALING WITH THE 1-3-1

The 1-3-1 zone is a unique and highly effective defense based on trapping and is used at all levels of the sport.

What makes the 1-3-1 devastating is its ability to eliminate passing lanes, "speed up" and panic ballhandlers and invite lob passes over the trap, right into areas where the defense is anticipating easy "interception" turnovers and fast break opportunities.

If you plan to use it on defense, I recommend these comprehensive guides:

- https://www.basketballforcoaches.com/1-3-1-zone-defense/
- https://www.breakthroughbasketball.com/defense/131-zone.html

BEATING THE 1-3-1

In youth hoops, against the 1-3-1 we walked the ball up using three guards. Two pass it back and forth between the middle lane and a sideline lane.

Our ball player invites the trap, then passes before it arrives. The 2-guard pass recipient then passes away from the trapping area — to the high post or opposite wing.

[Another go-to when playing against a one-man front in the 2-1-2 if you feel your two guards are good enough ballhandlers.]

AGAINST 1-3-1: The other way to beat it is an overload. Here's a look in the halfcourt:

This look would have started with 1 and 2 bringing the ball up and past timeline, with 3 and 4 working the high post (3) and corner/short corner (4). Have your 5 run the baseline, "mirroring" (following parallel) the ball. Or your 5 can work from the block to the corner. The short corner player (4) should always be open.

Finally, Tom Izzo and Michigan State are known for attacking and solving the 131 halfcourt look. Although a bit dated, this YouTube video of Izzo's Spartans attacking the 1-3-1 is gold:
https://www.youtube.com/watch?v=nV_LNGksWFk.

PRESS BREAK

Against a good diamond or Man press I used two plays to get my group out of trouble. Each one is easy to drill in practice. Rotate all your players in each position in these plays, so that in hectic, live-game conditions later they'll know what to do from any spot they end up standing in.

"GO"

In GO we send three players "behind" the pressing defenders, allowing our kids to make cuts with a player between them and the ball.

Don't forget that after a made basket [only], your inbounder can run side to side out of bounds.

Whoever receives the initial pass, tries to get it right back to the inbounder (who will be open). Bounce pass is a great option usually.

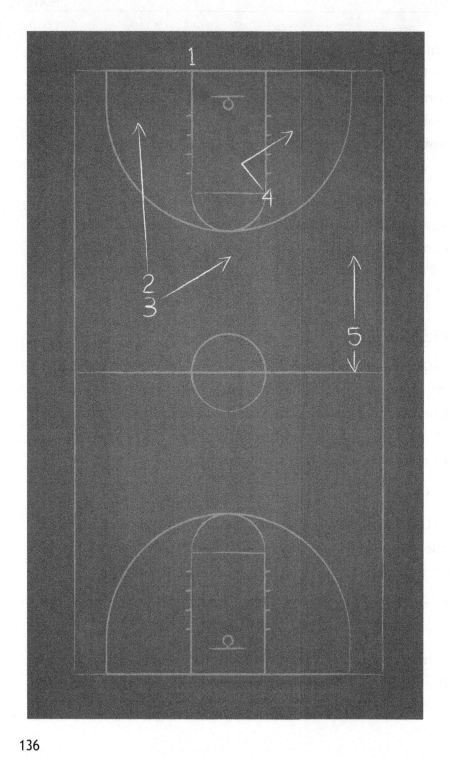

If 1 does get that pass back, 3 can now drop lower (i.e, behind 1) and be the "safety" as together 1, 2 and 4 bring the ball up. 5 would be heading to the paint.

"JAG"

Our other press-breaker works really well, most likely because it is easy for the players to remember. Put a 2-player stack right above midcourt, and put another 2-player stack just above the free throw line.

- On your inbounder's "ball slap" signal, both of your 2-player stacks sprint to the ball in different directions.
- The foul line duo splits out left and right into the defensive left- and right-side "short corners."
- The midcourt duo splits a little differently. The first (closer) player sprints up and hard to ball side. The back player sprints straight up the middle, and you're hoping for this pass. If it's not there, however, your inbounder has three other options.

Remember that the inbounder is permitted to run the baseline (if necessary) after a made basket by your opponent. Whoever gets the ball, they should time to gather and turn up the court, even if defended. Try to get the ball back to the inbounder, who should be available.

OVERTIME

"Be strong in body, clean in mind, lofty in ideals."

-DR. JAMES NAISMITH

OVERTIME

After publishing the first edition of **Coaching Youth Basketball** *in 2021, I realized I had numerous, additional thoughts and ideas to share.*

"That should be in the book, too!" was my mantra regarding these slightly off-topic or advanced items. I began corralling ideas in a document I nicknamed, "Overtime."

In the passage that follows you'll see these short additions. I hope that they too will help you on your coaching journey. I wish you great fun and success in coaching young players in this grand game of basketball!

– Stuart Wade, September 30, 2022

ANY TEAM ANY AGE CAN DEFEND—HARD

You can be as good a team as you want to be, if you DEFEND (and if on offense you value possessions/protect the ball). Ability, skill and technique of course are not the same for young to elementary to middle school age players. Here are three weapons useful to any-age defense:

- Pressure your man. Get up on him, in position based on his dribble-hand. Move your feet to defend and use outstretched/waving hands
- Raise your physicality. (No, this doesn't mean contact.) Run. Don't jog. Set a good screen, with intention. Get right up on your man on an inbounds play. Box out hard, go up and rip that rebound down
- Contest every shot. At no time in half-court allow the opposing player(s) an uncontested, free and clear shot. Every single attempt should have a defender in front of it, or arriving as fast as possible in close-out mode

ATTACK THE RIM

Do not allow your team to settle back and simply chuck jumpers from the perimeter. To win consistently, your group must also be able to:

- Attack the rim. [Take the ball to the hole]
- Draw fouls. [Be the aggressor when on offense]
- Hit free throws. [Emphasize it]

AVOID DOUBLING DOWN

A young ballhandler who has just turned over the ball is much more likely to commit an instant foul on the next defensive trip. In trying to get the ball back, the player is more willing to take a risk at this moment than at almost any other point in the game. Why? He's already in negative mental territory, after giving up possession, so he's now ready to overcompensate. Don't let your players commit this unnecessary double-down! So what to do about it? Cover this in practice. Have the group policing itself to "flush" mistakes and keep playing.

COMPETE

There's "Play Hard," and then there's "Compete." Which of your players is really competing and who is just playing hard? Players who compete do any/all of the following, in practice as well as during games:

- Fight for the rebound
- Contest the shot
- Dive for a loose ball
- Run back on defense

- Make hard cuts; on offense walk your man, then "explode cut"
- Work through (without fouling) the game's first screen that you face
- Embrace rather than withdraw from pressure
- Respond to setbacks (trailing, getting the ball taken, etc.) — Your reaction determines capacity for success
- Communicate, support, reinforce strategy (and one another)

There's nothing wrong with, "Play Hard!" Although the Compete vs. Play Hard difference may be slight, when you see someone competing, point it out for praise. Consider drills you could run (at age-appropriate levels) to instill hustle and effort beyond simply, "Play Hard!"

ENDGAME

Even late in a game you lead, it's still about good possessions, taking good shots, and stopping the other guy. Remember that an empty trip is the same as a turnover.

Late in the game, your better scorers will want to take matters into their own hands. That's a good thing, IF and only if you've already paid close attention to their previous decision-making and you've given them the green light.

Take pains to have productive possessions. Movement plus patience equals points. The ball has to move on offense. Do not allow crunch time to turn into "Me Ball" (too much dribbling, no passing, bull your way to the basket, take a tough/contested shot). Praise the good decisions and excise the bad ones.

GET BACK ON D

Guards need to remember to get back and protect against the fast break. If the opponent gets a defensive rebound, our players should harass the rebounder. Trap; try to strip ball (no foul!); face-guard him full-court to impede fast break opportunity. To succeed full-court, your group has to be in excellent cardio shape. Effort has to be maintained under fatigue more often now (or sub out for others). Option 1, get back quickly. Option 2, pressure the ball full court.

MAINTAIN ENERGY AS A GROUP

I have faced this situation too many times (surely you have, too): You are playing an athletic, respected opponent. Your squad is hanging tough, trailing by 3, now by 5... But, you're answering.

Your team hasn't led, but they're staying close. Your players are pestering the opposition and "hanging around" the supposedly "better" squad with plenty of time remaining.

Suddenly, however, the opponent scores two quick buckets to extend its lead to nine:

Now, our body language is sagging and we start to lose guys "off the back." Some are clearly no longer willing to stick with it, to keep on working to stay close.

This challenge is mental. How can this be fixed? What actions do we take and what (if any) personnel changes would be needed?

Ask yourself:
- Do we burn a precious timeout now (to re-set), or preserve it?

- Who will continue working and do what is needed — and more importantly, who won't? (Replace any player who seems to have had enough.)

- Who are our mudders? Which player(s) can be counted on right now to enter the game, providing hustle and adding energy? Every team has a super sub, that bench player who lifts his teammates and is 100% battle ready. (Send in that sparkplug player to get the jolt needed at this critical moment.)

NO FOULS WITH THE LEAD

Teams and players protecting a narrow lead, especially late in the game, have no business fouling — yet they often will.

Fouling negates effort. Two things you control as a group late in a game are: running clock on offense; and playing textbook defense, without allowing the clock to stop because of an unnecessary foul.

Defend without fouling!

- NOTE: For the slightly older players there's the trendy solution, "ALWAYS foul, up three late." I am not a fan of this action. In my opinion, at this age it is better to let the clock tick.

SAGE ADVICE

From Hall of Fame coaching legend Bob Knight, this is a simple but important concept that many overlook:

- Prevent your opponent from getting GOOD shots — "good" defined here as an uncontested, or high-percentage spot from the floor. Because your defense did

its job, you don't even give them the chance to shoot a block lay-up, or attempt a wide-open three, e.g.
- Meanwhile, work hard yourself to get those exact same GOOD shots on offense — and, DON'T TAKE "BAD" SHOTS. Coach Knight defines 'bad' here as: low-percentage jump shot from way out, a heavily contested shot (especially when a teammate is open/closer), or an off-balance or "not set" jumper, etc.

SPACING

Kids need to know the importance of spacing and awareness off/away from the ball. Success on offense in the half-court comes when you take your time, when the offensive players have good spacing and good ball movement (penetrate, kick-out, take and hit the open shot). Sequences that end with that extra pass being made, followed by the knockdown of an "even better" open shot, simply because the ball moved... Fun to watch!

WARMUPS ARE ABOUT US... AND ONLY US

Politely, firmly discourage your team from watching the opposing team warm-up before the game starts. (It'll be near impossible but do it anyway.)

Tell them instead that the coaches will pay attention, on behalf of the team, to watch their warm-up and report anything of note that you saw.

Teams and individuals can get beaten mentally (and then, for real, after tipoff) during pregame warm-ups, just by seeing good outside shooters or other skillful maneuvers on display.

It's critical that you focus your team on its own preparation.

Find a way to convey: What the other team is doing simply does not matter. The only approach that matters is ours. If the opponents want to watch us warm up and get worried, that's their choice.

WHAT TO SAY BEFORE THE BIG GAME

There's no right or wrong script; hope this helps:

Is anybody nervous? It's alright to be nervous; the other team is too. If you didn't feel a little nervous, it wouldn't be the right feeling, right now. What should you do about it?

Breathe. It's just a basketball game. To get rid of that pre-game, jittery feeling all you really have to do is — **Do your job**:
- Same terrific effort, intensity, and execution as ever
- Positive talk, flush any mistake and move on
- Leader on the court, find your mental calm place in the chaos

Walk in, warm up and **play tonight with high confidence** in yourself, and in this team.
- You have earned your way and you deserve to be here.

Let's go do what we do! LET'S GO TAKE THE WIN.

A final thought — this one on the subject of courage— from the immortal Harvey Dorfman: *"Courage is often required to act against fatigue. A courageous competitor does not allow natural decrease over time of his level of physical energy to diminish his mental energy. Suck It Up. And do not, ever, disappear."*

*****

THE ALPHA AND THE OMEGA: DEFENSE

I leave you with this thought: Don't just get good on defense… **BE GREAT ON DEFENSE.**

SELECT/KEY RULES OF THE GAME

The rules of basketball are widely available online. For best results if you are new to the game, consult the specific set of rules distributed by your league, and applicable to the specific games you will be involved in. For a sense of those at the youngest, youth level, I recommend looking at your local YMCA website, searching for "Youth Basketball Rules." There, you'll find the latest sanctioned set of current YMCA rules by age range.

Here's a select set of some of the essential and commonly misunderstood rules of the game:

Held Ball (AKA Tie-up, or Jump Ball)

A held ball occurs when two or more players from opposing teams are in possession of the ball, and control cannot be obtained without undue roughness. At the professional, college, and high school levels, possession is decided with a jump ball. In youth leagues, however, possession commonly is decided by the possession arrow at the scorer's table. In some leagues, possession following a held ball alternates from one team to the other.

3-Second Rule

An offensive player must move out of the lane, key, or paint (the rectangular area designated on the court between the foul line and the end line) before 3 seconds elapse. In the event of a violation, the ball is awarded to the team on defense. There is no 3-second restriction for defensive players.

Carrying or Palming

Carrying, or palming, is a violation that occurs when an offensive player dribbles the ball so that it rests and stays in the palm of the hand.

Backcourt Violation

After a made basket, the team that is now moving to offense has ten seconds to move the ball across midcourt. The stripe here is also known as the timeline, half-court line, centerline or midline. In addition, once the offense brings the ball over the midcourt line, the offense cannot go back across the line. If the ball does cross the line, the other team gets possession. If the offense is making an inbounds pass on the side, they can pass it back over the line, however.

Personal Fouls

A personal foul is any type of illegal contact, including slapping, holding, pushing, or hitting. Personal fouls are most often committed on an offensive player by a defender, although an offensive player can foul a defender as well.

Other personal fouls include these three: reaching in, a defender reaches in to steal the ball and makes contact with the dribbler; over the back, a player jumps over the back of the opposition on a rebound; illegal pick, a player tries to set a pick but either moves his feet or throws an elbow, making contact with the opposition.

Charging (offensive foul)

This offensive foul (a foul committed by the team with the ball) consists of illegal personal contact by pushing or moving into an opponent's torso, most likely when an offensive player drives to the basket and "runs over" a defensive player.

Moving Screen (offensive foul)

When screening, the screener should jump-stop and hold that position. Once a screener sets a screen, he may not lean into the defender—he must be stationary, otherwise this is an offensive "moving screen" violation and a personal foul.

Blocking Foul

A blocking foul is illegal personal contact that impedes the progress of an opponent, most likely when a defensive player "bodies" an offensive player who is driving to the hoop.

Flagrant Foul

A flagrant foul involves excessively physical contact with an opponent, including punching, kneeing, or kicking.

Intentional Foul

An intentional foul occurs when the player is not directly going for or playing the ball. A common situational example:

My team trails by 1 or more with less than a minute to play. We try for the steal, but we don't get it, so we have our defender place two hands on the offensive ball-handler. This is an intentional foul we expend — It stops the clock, and puts their player most likely at the foul line to shoot. Strategically we "trade" a potential score for them, with a stopped clock that we need to extend the basketball game for a few more seconds.

Technical Foul

A technical foul is a violation committed by either a player or a coach. It involves no contact with an opponent or contact while the ball is dead. Examples include vulgarity, profanity, or obscene gestures.

ABOUT THE AUTHOR

Getting in some work, 2013. The author on the left, with his sons John (#3) and Rob at far right.

Stuart Wade is a writer, marketing consultant, and former technology communications executive. He is the author of three books, and writes about business, technology and culture. Stu is equally at ease writing for corporate clients as for stand-up comedians, and appreciates the similarities between the two. A devoted husband and father of three boys, the Austin, Texas resident holds a journalism degree from Indiana University.

ALSO BY THE AUTHOR

Tacoma Rail: 100 Years and Still on Track (Donning, 2016)

Drop Us a Line… Sucker (Carrol & Graf, 1995)

ACKNOWLEDGMENTS

- The YMCA of Austin
- West Austin Youth Association (WAYA)
- Breakthrough Basketball
- *Toughness* by Jay Bilas
- Bow River Basketball
- Northwest Austin Youth Basketball Association (NWAYBA)
- Positive Coaching Alliance
- Coaches Clipboard
- *Relentless* by Tim Grover
- *Coaching The Mental Game* by H.A. Dorfman
- *Intentional Mindset* by Dave Anderson

Rules-page source: Faucher, David G. The Baffled Parent's Guide to Coaching Youth Basketball (2000)

Special thanks to Steven Dietz, Randy Varela and David Clark

Thanks also to many coaching friends: Munir Ahamed, Mike Armour, Dustin Armstrong, Ron Baxter, Chris Brown, David Clemons, Bill Cooper, Tim Duncan, Jim Dunham, Daniel Fuentes, Brandon Greene, Phil Henderson, Alex Inman, Kendall Isom, Adam Jones, Eric Krell, Mike Palmer, Carlin Shaw, Terry Smothers, David Spradling, Joe Strathmann, Adam Venn, Mark Wagner, Stuart Whitlow and many more spanning YMCA, WAYA, NWAYBA, AAU, IHSAA and UIL basketball. Thank you!

Made in United States
North Haven, CT
12 December 2023

45564984R00095